Church
and
World

CHURCH AND WORLD

The Unity of the Church and the Renewal of Human Community

A Faith and Order Study Document

Faith and Order Paper No. 151

WCC Publications, Geneva

Cover design: Rob Lucas

ISBN 2-8254-1004-7

© 1990 WCC Publications, World Council of Churches,
150, route de Ferney, 1211 Geneva 2, Switzerland

Printed in Switzerland

Table of Contents

Preface

The relationship between efforts towards manifesting the unity of the church and efforts towards common Christian witness and service in the world has, from the beginning, occupied an important place on the ecumenical agenda. There have been repeated affirmations that these two efforts should be held together — and equally frequent statements, and actions, which set one against the other. The Commission on Faith and Order of the World Council of Churches (WCC) has taken up this challenge by initiating, at its meeting in Lima, Peru, in 1982, a study programme on The Unity of the Church and the Renewal of Human Community.

The study document presented here is a first result of this programme. It integrates the results of seven international consultations — in Africa, Asia, the Caribbean, both Eastern and Western Europe, Latin America and North America — focussing on specific aspects of Unity and Renewal, contributions from local study groups, continued reflection by the Unity and Renewal Steering Group and advisors, and review by the Faith and Order Standing and Plenary Commissions. This process was pursued from 1984-1989.

The initial version of this text was produced, after preliminary drafting, at a meeting of the Unity and Renewal Steering Group together with advisers at Leuenberg, Switzerland, in March 1989; this was carefully reviewed by the Faith and Order Plenary Commission at its meeting in Budapest in August 1989. On the basis of suggestions by the Plenary Commission at Budapest, the text was revised at a consultation of the Unity and Renewal Steering Group and advisers in Mandeville, Jamaica in January 1990. The text was given final form, and approved "for publication, distribution, and study by the churches", at the meeting of the Faith and Order Standing Commission in Dunblane, Scotland, in August 1990.

The text reflects the contributions of many persons from different theological perspectives and varied cultural backgrounds who, each in close touch with his or her own tradition, have struggled to find what can be said together today about God's call to the churches to seek unity and to be signs and instruments of the renewal of the human community. The text is, therefore, an expression of ecumenical convergence on these issues, to be studied and "tested" by the churches as a help and impetus for their own self-understanding and their common efforts towards unity and renewal.

We are happy that the study on The Unity of the Church and the Renewal of Human Community, which had to struggle with difficult theological and methodological questions (and which will be continued in the coming years), has led to this important first result. We are convinced that this text, and the churches' reflection upon it, will also be of great significance for the Faith and Order World Conference in 1993.

Our deep gratitude is due to all who have contributed to the unity and renewal programme and to the elaboration of this text. We thank especially Dr. Paul A. Crow, Jr., Moderator of the Unity and Renewal Steering Group, for his skillful and committed leadership of the study process; and Dr. Thomas F. Best, the Faith and Order Executive Secretary responsible for the study, for his untiring and creative staff work on its many aspects.

We are now submitting this study document to the churches for their study and as a means by which, if God wills, they may be led forward on the way to their unity within God's purpose for all humankind.

        John Deschner, Moderator   Günther Gassmann, Director

                        Commission on Faith and Order
                            Geneva, October 1990

CHAPTER I

Introduction:
The Vision and Process of the
Study on Unity and Renewal

1. The Human Situation and the Christian Response: The Setting of the Study

1. Today the world — with its many diverse cultures, peoples, historical legacies and present situations — is marked by opportunities and dangers, hopes and anxieties. Many of these are local, related to particular areas and issues; many are becoming more and more global in their scope and implications. There is a deep yearning for meaning, for justice, peace, and the preservation of the resources of life, which is shared by millions of people and which is echoed by the yearnings of all creatures (Rom. 8:18-25).* There is the pain of hunger and broken hopes, the suffering of those whose human rights are violated, of the victims of racism and sexism, of the exploited and the oppressed and the poor.

2. Yet there are other, more hopeful dimensions. There are growing commitments to peace and human rights, to a right economic development and to the beneficial use of science and technology; there are the positive efforts of many international organizations to reduce human suffering; there are the deep yearnings and commitments of many persons and groups for meaning in life, for reconciliation, for the wholeness of creation. Christians welcome with gratitude the striving of all persons of goodwill to move beyond brokenness and division toward new wholeness and unity. But Christians are also aware of the ambivalence and partiality of all human endeavours.

3. Christians and churches live in the world, in the midst of these anxieties and hopes. They share in them and are challenged by them, while at the same time they are not "of" the world, viewing it always from the unique, life-giving perspective of the gospel. Christians live, fundamentally, from the blessings

---

*Biblical texts generally follow the rendering of the Revised Standard Version; the New Revised Standard Version, which became available towards the end of the study process, has been followed in a few cases.

of Christ's cross and resurrection; they affirm, in the power of the Spirit, that God's saving action creates a hope for unity and renewal, for justice and reconciliation that can never be destroyed.

4. The people of God, who in the power of the Holy Spirit confess Jesus Christ as God, Lord and Saviour, are called and sent to struggle for renewal and life in this world marked by sin, suffering and death. To neglect so to do is for the church to deny its own nature and calling to be a prophetic sign for the world, and to become "conformed to this world". Despite the fact that human sin will continue to create division and injustice, the church proclaims that through the mystery of Christ's life, death and resurrection, life will be victorious over death, that human divisions may be overcome and reconciliation achieved. In the celebration of the eucharist the church challenges all forms of injustice (*Baptism, Eucharist and Ministry*, Eucharist, para. 20; cf. in the present text Chapter IV, para. 31). The church continues to speak a prophetic word, confronting oppression and injustice with the affirmation that "Satan, your kingdom must come down!" (Harlem Consultation Report, p. 6; *Mid-Stream*, XXVIII, 4, p. 417; cf. Mark 3:26).*

5. Christians and the churches, however, are also marked by differences. They follow different traditions and have different understandings of the nature, identity and boundaries of the church. They sometimes disagree about whether, and in what ways, the churches should involve themselves in specific social issues. To the extent that these differences divide them and hinder their common proclamation, witness and service, the churches are challenged to dialogue and shared life, to a search for mutual understanding and common perspectives which can enable them to overcome their ecclesial divisions, and to realize and embody that unity which is God's gracious gift. In faithfulness to God's call, and for the fulfilment of their vocation, the churches seek that unity for which Jesus prayed. This is a unity not only visible to the world but also of a spiritual authenticity as a communion of prayer, worship and *diakonia* (service) which can help the world to respond to God in faith (cf. Chapter III, para. 10).

6. Christians confess the church as willed by God, the body of Christ, a reality transcending time and space and prefiguring the kingdom of God which is to come, and experience at the same time the historical and human reality of the church as institution, as visible communities of believers existing each in a particular time and place. In the course of history the life of the church has been marked by the effective action of God's grace, producing much that is good and holy. But faithfulness to the gospel calls Christians to recognize distortions in the historical life of the church. The church too stands under

---

*The Consultation Reports and other materials cited in the Study Document are listed in Appendix 1, pp. 80-86. Reports are available from the Faith and Order Secretariat, World Council of Churches, P. O. Box 2100, 1211 Geneva 2, Switzerland. Full documentations of the consultations are available from the World Council of Churches Bookshop at the same address. For additional related titles see "Unity and Renewal — A Working Bibliography", 26 July 1990, available from Faith and Order.

> Today, conversion to God (*metanoia*) means a commitment to seeking ways
>
> ...out of the divisions in which the churches continue to live,
> ...out of the suspicion and hostility in their mutual relations,
> ...out of the burden of paralysing memories of the past,
> ...out of intolerance and the refusal to recognise religious freedom,
>
> Into a community which recognises its needs to be constantly forgiven and renewed and together gives praise to God for his love and gifts.
>
> European Ecumenical Assembly, Basel, 1989

the judgment of the word of God, and in its human and historical reality is called to repentance and renewal. It is called "to become what it is", to embody in its historical and institutional life its true nature as a holy, reconciled and reconciling community. Thus in responding to its divine mandate the church must strive, through the power of the Spirit, to struggle within its own historical life against all marks of brokenness, division and injustice — oppressive structures, abuses of power, discrimination based on race, sex or caste, excessive individualism — all that divides Christians from one another.

7. This striving is not for the sake of the church alone. It is in and for the world that God calls the church that it may be a sign and bearer of the Triune God's work towards the salvation and renewal of all humankind. Thus the church participates in the mystery and mission of God, and thereby can be understood as mystery and prophetic sign.

2. Overcoming an Ecumenical Polarization: the Goal of the Study

8. This study of the World Council of Churches Faith and Order Commission on The Unity of the Church and the Renewal of Human Community affirms and explores the inter-relation of two fundamental ecumenical tasks: the search for the visible unity of Christ's Church, and the search for common Christian proclamation, witness and service as expressions of God's mission and love for a world crying out for renewal.

9. The term "visible unity" is understood in the sense of the first constitutional function and purpose of the WCC: "to call the churches to the goal of visible unity in one faith and in one eucharistic fellowship expressed in worship and in common life in Christ, and to advance towards that unity in order that the world may believe" (WCC Constitution, III, "Functions and Purposes", 1; cf. in the present text Chapter IV, para. 31). The term "renewal", which is applied and described in different contexts in the present document, points to the saving and transforming action of the Triune God

for creation, church and humanity. Renewal, in this sense, seeks to heal and to transcend the limitations, ambiguities and destructive divisions of a world which is, theologically speaking, fallen. (This fallen condition of the world is frequently indicated in this study by the term "brokenness".) Christians are called to serve this dynamic process of God's drawing all people into a reconciled life in Christ through the Holy Spirit.

10. These two issues — the search for unity and the search for renewal — are often seen as being separate and distinct, and with this goes the tendency to consider either one *or* the other as the most important or urgent ecumenical task. This contradicts, however, the long-held ecumenical conviction that God's will, revealed in Jesus Christ, calls the churches both to visible unity among themselves and to common witness and service for the renewal of human community. By explicating theologically this ecumenical conviction, this study seeks to respond to a fundamental ecumenical issue by indicating not only that, but also how, these two ecumenical tasks are indissolubly inter-related.

11. This attempt has led inevitably to a broader ecumenical reflection on the church (and not only on the more specific issue of the visible unity of the church). Thus the goal of the study concentrates on the questions: How can the church be understood in such a way that the nature of the church, and the mission of the church, are seen as integral and inter-related elements of the being (the *esse*) of the church itself? How can the inter-relation between the church, thus conceived, and humanity "outside" the church be understood — beyond their obvious relation, following from the fact that the church lives in the world and is sent to the world — in a coherent theological perspective? Does the kingdom of God, within the wider framework of the triune God's plan of salvation from creation to new creation, offer such a perspective?

12. This broader ecclesiological approach represents a new step in ecumenical reflection, but certainly not yet a comprehensive ecclesiology in an ecumenical perspective. This task is still before us. The study has tried to include various ecclesiological images and themes, and has fostered the interaction of different ecclesiological approaches: namely those which begin from the unique divine identity and holiness of the church, and those which begin from the church as an historical reality and from its calling to serve God's purpose of healing, reconciliation and justice among humankind.

13. To develop this theological (and especially ecclesiological) understanding of the inter-relation between Church and humanity not only in general, but also to exemplify it in a more concrete manner, two specific issues — the concerns for justice and for the community of women and men — were chosen from the wide range of human and social issues crying out for renewal. In making this choice Faith and Order does not seek to do ecumenical social ethics by studying these two issues as such; this does not belong directly to its mandate and competence. But the study may, nevertheless, also contribute to the urgent task of re-considering basic lines of ecumenical social ethics.

3. Steps on the Way: the Process Towards this Study Document

14. From its beginning the Faith and Order Commission has seen its work towards the visible manifestation of the unity already given to the church in Jesus Christ as a contribution to the movement towards common Christian witness and service in the world. From this perspective the concern for the visible unity of the church is understood as the common obedience of Christians to the saving purpose of the Triune God for all humanity in creation, redemption and fulfilment.

15. The study on Unity and Renewal continues and develops earlier work done in Faith and Order, especially the studies on The Unity of the Church and the Unity of Humankind, and The Community of Women and Men in the Church (the latter "lodged" in Faith and Order and done jointly with the WCC sub-unit on Women in Church and Society). It is the result of decisions taken at the Faith and Order Plenary Commission meeting in Lima, Peru (1982). In affirming this study the WCC Sixth Assembly in Vancouver in 1983 emphasized that it should have, in accordance with the general orientation of all Faith and Order work, an ecclesiological focus, making "a theological exploration of the church as 'sign' a central part of [this] programme..." (*Gathered for Life*, p. 50; cf. *Nairobi to Vancouver*, pp. 77, 84.).* Those planning the WCC's work after the Vancouver Assembly noted the "strategic importance" of the project as "an overall concern and coordinating perspective for the Council as a whole" (Report of the Core Group on Unit I [Montreux, 1984], p. 1).

...God's will, revealed in Jesus Christ, calls the churches both to visible unity among themselves and to common witness and service for the renewal of human community

---

16. The exploration of ecclesiology in this study takes special account of the theological inter-relation between the unity of the church and the renewal of its life, and the mission and calling of the church to be God's instrument in efforts for renewal of the human community. Because faithful response to the gospel involves the "doing" of faith in concrete acts of proclamation, mission and service, this study has sought to discern the ecclesiological significance of the experience of Christians who are witnessing, in specific situations, to the meaning and consequences of the gospel for their own time and place.

---

*This ecclesiological focus was sharpened at the Faith and Order Standing Commission meeting on Crete (1984), and has been reviewed and developed at meetings of the Faith and Order Plenary and Standing Commissions, and the Unity and Renewal Steering Group, as indicated in the respective *Minutes* (Stavanger, 1985; Potsdam, 1986; Madrid, 1987; Boston, 1988; Budapest, 1989; Dunblane, 1990).

17. Accordingly the study on Unity and Renewal has been developed towards the integration of four elements. The *first* element is the exploration of several theological and ecclesiological themes which have proven helpful in reflecting on the nature of the church and its unity in relation to its calling to proclamation, mission and service in the world. These are:

— the kingdom of God, the biblical vision of the creative, redeeming and sustaining rule of God;

— the church as mystery, with its emphasis upon the reality of the church as divine body of Christ;

— the church as prophetic sign, with its emphasis upon the church as instrument of God's grace given to a world crying out for healing and renewal;

— an overarching eschatological and doxological affirmation, which places all human reflection and action in the perspective of the certain final realization of God's saving purpose for all humankind.

18. Biblical and theological perspectives on these themes were explored in a consultation at Chantilly, France (1985);* the resulting text on "The Church as Mystery and Prophetic Sign" has been extensively developed and is incorporated in this study document, primarily in Chapters II (material on the kingdom) and III (material on the church as mystery and as prophetic sign). The eschatological and doxological focus has been developed in Chapter VII as the conclusion to the study document as a whole.

19. The second and third elements of the Study are two areas which have been chosen to exemplify the inter-relation between church and humanity in the perspective of specific issues of unity and renewal. In each case a series of consultations has combined biblical and theological presentations with reflections upon the theological and ecclesiological significance of Christian life and witness in specific contexts. These consultations have been concerned not with these issues in themselves but with their implications for the nature of the church and its proclamation, mission and service today.

20. The *second* element is reflection upon the ecclesiological implications of the church's involvement in issues of justice. Three consultations have explored this theme in varied contexts (Singapore, 1986; Porto Alegre, Brazil, 1987; Harlem, USA, 1988); their results and insights were integrated by the Steering Group at its meeting in Boston in 1988, and have been incorporated into Chapter IV of this text.

21. The *third* element is reflection upon the ecclesiological significance of the search for a more complete and authentic community of women and men. This has been explored in two consultations (Prague, 1985; Porto Novo, Benin, 1988); their results and insights were integrated at a consultation of

---

*The Unity and Renewal consultations and Faith and Order Commission/Steering Group meetings are given in Appendices 2 and 3, pp. 87-88.

Steering Group members and advisors in Cambridge, U.K. in 1989, and have been integrated into Chapter V of this text.

22. Common insights emerged from the consultations on the second and third elements of the study about life in Christian community, and about language and power in particular. These form part of Chapter VI of this text.

23. Thus these three elements have formed the basis of this Study Document on Unity and Renewal. A *fourth* element in the study programme has been the process of reflection in local groups around the world. This is intended to help Faith and Order listen to insights and experience from the level of the local congregation.* Christians around the world have been invited to address issues of unity and renewal from the perspective of their own experience and that of their Christian community, using the text *Unity and Renewal: A Study Guide for Local Groups* as a stimulus and guide for reflection and discussion. Available reports have been reviewed at meetings of the Steering Group and advisors (especially at the Cambridge, U.K. meeting in 1988); but the process had not advanced sufficiently for the reflections and experience from the study groups to interact significantly with the present text.

24. It is fitting that the Unity and Renewal study process, with its many parts and its combination of theological approaches and methods, should result in a study document which is not only theologically substantial but also lively in presentation and accessible to the reader. Sentences from the text itself are sometimes repeated, in larger type and between horizontal lines, to give focus or emphasis. Some additional "illustrative" material — testimonies from the lives of Christians and Christian communities, quotations from sources both ancient and modern — has also been included to focus points made in the text, to link the text with the past and present experience of other Christians, and to place the text within the context of the broader ecumenical movement. This is enclosed within a box to separate it from the text proper. *Such material is not part of the official text of this Study Document.*

4. An Invitation to Study and Reflection

25. This study has depended both upon theological reflection on the church as mystery and prophetic sign and upon theological reflection on the contextual study of the implications, for the understanding of the church and its unity, of the concerns for justice and for the community of women and men. At times these approaches have seemed to be separate and even contradictory; in the process of the study it has become evident that they can enter into creative interaction, so that the results of the reflection on the themes of mystery and prophetic sign can be reaffirmed — and with deeper understanding — when they are seen in close relation to the contextual studies.

---

*As foreseen in the Faith and Order Commission *Minutes* from Crete (pp. 39-40), Stavanger, 1985 (pp. 211-214), Potsdam, 1986 (pp. 44-45), Madrid, 1987 (pp. 84-85), and Boston (pp. 12-13, 97-98).

26. This study document proposes elements of an ecumenical convergence on the understanding of the church and its relation to the wider human community. Therefore it seeks to help the churches discern common and converging ecclesiological perspectives in their understanding of the church in its relation to unity and renewal. It invites them to consider, both individually and together, the affirmation that the visible unity of Christ's church, and the renewal of human community, are both rooted in the Triune God's will and are therefore closely inter-related; and to consider the implications of this affirmation for the faith, order, life and witness of the church in each place and for the churches together on their pilgrimage towards visible unity.

27. Questions have been given at the end of each chapter to focus the practical implications of the material, and to invite the reader into conversation with the text — and with others in his or her own church or Christian community. They are offered to stimulate and orient the study and discussion of the text in churches, ecumenical commissions and groups, theological seminaries, and elsewhere. The questions on page 10 following this introductory chapter relate to the study document as a whole, and readers may wish to return to them after reading the entire text.

28. Although the study document is intended in the first place to help churches and Christian groups in their own reflection and ecumenical relationships, Faith and Order would be most interested in their reflections and comments upon it. These should be sent to the Faith and Order Secretariat at the World Council of Churches, 1211 Geneva 2, Switzerland.

29. Such a response would be most helpful for Faith and Order's continuing work. Its Standing Commission has already made preliminary proposals for the future of the study, including work on other specific aspects of the inter-relation between the church and the wider human community (for example, issues of nationalism, or culture and inculturation). Thus the Faith and Order study on the Unity of the Church and the Renewal of Human Community will continue; the participation of the churches in this on-going process will be of crucial significance, and will be warmly welcomed.

Questions for Reflection and Discussion:
The Study Document as a Whole

1. Do you find the description of the church as instrument and foretaste of the kingdom helpful for your understanding of the life and task of the church today?

2. Are the search for the visible unity of the church, and the struggle for the renewal of human community, inter-related in your church?

3. In your experience, what is the difference between life in Christian community and life in the human community in general?

4. What consequences can you draw from this study document for your own situation?

An African Bishop's Story

An illiterate old woman reflecting on the Eucharist confronted me with a serious theological argument and asked some serious questions. She told me that since the priest of her own denomination could visit their congregation only once a month, she sometimes went to the service at another church since their priest (who had a car) was able to visit there more often. She said:

> On one such occasion Father X visited and that morning I felt spiritually hungry so I went to the other service. When it was time for Holy Communion I felt I should partake, so I got up to go to the altar. The priest, who knew me personally and also knew that I am from another church, sent one of the servers to tell me not to go for Communion.
>
> I was not only embarrassed but I felt spiritually rejected and let down. What worries me is that when there was a shortage of food in 1984, Father X brought rice and beans to this village and when I went to the Mission House, he gave me enough rice and beans to last me and my family for about two weeks. And yet when I got up to go for Communion he refused me.
>
> Bishop, I do not believe that you Bishops, priests and ministers make the things of the altar holy, they are made holy by God. Is the Jesus you clergymen preach the same Jesus who went about doing good, the Jesus who received the Samaritan woman, Mary Magdalene, the publican Zacchaeus, the Jesus who was a friend of publicans and sinners? I do not believe that the Lord himself would have refused me.

The old lady concluded by saying, "May God's Kingdom come quickly and then we will know who is right".

T. S. A. Annobil of Ghana

CHAPTER II

Unity and Renewal
in the Light of the Kingdom

1. The two issues of "unity" and "renewal" as briefly described in Chapter I are intimately related. Moreover they apply, each in a particular way, both to "church" and to "human community". To delineate the inter-relation of unity and renewal to church and human community, the perspective of the kingdom is fundamental. This chapter discusses the announcement of the kingdom, the response which it evokes and the promise of life which it brings. It has been recognised in this study that the English word "kingdom" is not always a good translation for the Greek word *basileia*, and also that the image of *basileia* should be understood in the context of other biblical images and of the other main themes of trinitarian theology.

1. The Announcement of the Kingdom

A. THE OLD TESTAMENT

2. The motif of the kingdom of God is one of the central themes of the prophetic message. Its understanding is anchored deeply in the Old Testament. Emphasis on the theme of God as the eschatological king and judge flourished during the period when Israel was influenced and occupied by foreign powers.

3. Interpreting the situation of Israel as due to its disobedience of God's commandments in its political and ethical decision-making (Deut. 30:11-20), the prophets announced the "Day of the Lord" as a day of "wrath" and "retribution" against injustice and immorality (Isa. 2:12-21, 61:2; Jer. 46:10; Zeph. 1:14-18).

4. However, wrath and retribution are not in themselves the goal of God's judgment. Rather the judgment of God is meant to establish again and anew what is right and just, to establish the kingdom of God before the eyes of Israel and the world. A new covenant between God and the people will be accomplished (Jer. 31:31-34), a covenant which will affect all the nations of

the world (Isa. 11:9, 56:7). A restored community will come into being and peace, justice and harmony will be experienced (Isa. 25:8, 32:17; Jer. 23:6; Ezek. 34:25; Hos. 2:20-23).

5. The reign of God will be eternal and universal. The Old Testament witnesses know that Yahweh is the true king of Israel and praise God as the ultimate authority not only for the people of God but for the whole creation: "The Lord is high above all nations, and his glory above the heavens" (Ps. 113:4). However bleak the horizons of the people of God and of the world in history, the recollection of the eschatological kingdom becomes the source of hope. God indeed is already "enthroned" today as yesterday, but the complete revelation of God's rule is still to come. God has the final word. The future belongs to God.

B. THE KINGDOM OF GOD IN THE LIFE AND MINISTRY OF JESUS OF NAZARETH

6. The prophetic message of the liberating sovereignty of God is fully taken up in the gospel of Jesus, which also challenged contemporary views of the kingdom. The way of Jesus cannot be understood apart from the eschatological note which is fundamental to it. The presupposition of his teaching and healing is that the final, decisive hour has already arrived: "The time is fulfilled, and the kingdom of God is at hand; repent and believe in the gospel" (Mark 1:15). The New Testament witnesses in their diverse voices confirm unanimously, in the light of Easter, that this presupposition holds true: in the person and story of Jesus of Nazareth, the sovereignty of God has once and for all definitively "become flesh". In Jesus, God's kingdom was — and is — "in our midst" (cf. Luke 17:21). The reality of the kingdom is embodied in the person and work of Jesus Christ, crucified and risen. Jesus' message is, fundamentally, the good news of the coming kingdom of God, of the liberating promise and claim of that kingdom.

1) The Message of Jesus

7. The message of Jesus is frequently conveyed in parables. Often the hearers of Jesus are encouraged to engage with the telling of the parable so that they are challenged to decide for themselves whether or not to accept the kingly rule of God. Most of the parables are centred on the mystery of the kingdom and the element of surprise is very common.

8. The Sermon on the Mount gathers much which conveys the essence of the kingdom. There are many different interpretations of the Sermon on the Mount. It has been called the covenantal constitution of the kingdom. In the Beatitudes, Jesus promised the happiness of the kingdom to those who know that they are in need: to the poor, the hungry, the weeping, the hated (Luke 6:20-23); and to the poor in spirit, those who mourn, the meek, those who hunger and thirst for righteousness, the merciful, the pure in heart, the peacemakers, those who are persecuted for righteousness' sake (Matt. 5:3-12).

2) The Mighty Acts of Jesus

9. Along with his words, the deeds of Jesus make the reign of God a present reality. This is clear, for example, in his healing miracles: these were understood as signs of the kingdom of God, not only by outsiders but also by Jesus himself: "If it is by the Spirit of God that I cast out demons, then the kingdom of God has indeed come upon you" (Matt. 12:28). Furthermore, and deeper still, the rule of God is realized not only in the action of Jesus but also in his Easter destiny, in his cross and resurrection. The unmistakable testimony of the New Testament is that in the way of Jesus of Nazareth, from the manger to the cross and to the empty tomb, the kingdom of God has dawned upon us. Jesus not only teaches, but also embodies and exemplifies what he taught.

2. The Response to the Kingdom

10. The early Christians' own immediate experience of kingdoms and kingship was the oppressive rule of the Herodians and their Roman masters. Yet with bold vision and faith they proclaimed a kingdom whose Lord is the suffering servant, whose life had been "poured out for many for the forgiveness of sins" in anticipation of the kingdom (Matt. 26:28-29). The shepherd-king of this flock is the Lamb "bearing the marks of slaughter", whose sacrificial death has made his followers "a kingdom" (Rev. 5:6-10); the messiah who inaugurates and embodies the reign of God is Christ Jesus in the power of the Spirit, who had "emptied himself" of his divine glory, "taking the form of a servant" (Phil. 2:7). Within such a kingdom domination has no place, and authority is expressed in service: in contrast to the kingdoms of this world, where "great men exercise authority over them", in the kingdom of God "whoever would be first among you must be servant of all" (Mark 10:42-44).

11. What are the consequences of the coming of God's kingdom for the ordering of human lives? The key statement of the message of Jesus points the way: "The kingdom of God is at hand, repent and believe in the gospel" (Mark 1:15). Here the indicative of the first sentence here is matched by the imperative of the second. The decisive concepts are "repentance" — or conversion of heart and life (*metanoia*) — and "faith".

A. THE CALL TO CONVERSION

12. It is instructive that the first word of the "appropriate" response to the coming kingdom of God should be the word "repent". This is anything but obvious. In the history of the interpretation of the kingdom of God, the kingdom has all too easily been understood as an extension of human ideals, the ultimate climax of human aspiration. The New Testament takes a quite different view. The kingdom of God passes a sovereign judgment on all human actions and plans, calling for conversion to a new life in union with God.

13. So in hearing the Word proclaimed and in receiving the Sacraments, each person and every community is judged by the revelation of the kingdom of

God. Persons and communities always fall short of what is being asked of them; thus they need continually to be called to repentance. The "good news" is that at the cross there is a place where all may lay their shortcomings and receive forgiveness.

B. THE CALL TO FAITH AND RENEWAL

14. The message of the kingdom of God is not only the summons to conversion; it is at the same time the summons to faith: "... and *believe in* the gospel". The gospel of the kingdom is certainly soberly aware of the reality of judgment and makes no secret of the seriousness of the human predicament; yet it does this not wavering between "yes" and "no", light and darkness, but as gospel, as good news, bringing with it hope. It is the word of promise and the reality of God's gift, the invitation to faith and to life in light of the promise.

15. The "good news" of the kingdom means not only forgiveness but also renewal. The Christ who forgives renews Christians and Christian communities. The power of the Holy Spirit touches persons and communities within the church for the renewal of their lives and their ministry and mission.

16. The Spirit which empowers and renews is the same Spirit which was upon Jesus in the dramatic events described in Luke 4:14-21, in the course of which Jesus says:

> The Spirit of the Lord is upon me, because he has anointed me to preach good news to the poor. He has sent me to proclaim release to the captives and recovery of sight to the blind, to set at liberty those who are oppressed, to proclaim the acceptable year of the Lord (Luke 4:18).

This is a quotation from the prophet Isaiah (61:1-2), sounding the basic affirmation of Israel's hope, the promise of God's liberating, reconciling future. On this text Jesus preaches his sermon, which Luke represents in one succinct sentence: "Today this scripture has been fulfilled in your hearing" (Luke 4:21). What Isaiah has promised as God's final messianic future is now operative. The promises set before humankind challenge and open up each concrete situation. Accordingly, discipleship in the kingdom of God consists in patient and persistent efforts to match human circumstances with God's promises, and God's promises with human circumstances. Such discipleship continuing in the faith and mission of the apostles equips Christians and their communities for worship, witness and service. So renewal begins with the members of the church; but it is never for themselves alone. The renewal of the church is always for the sake of the human community, for which the church is a sign and foretaste of that kingdom of God which comes to us both as judgment and as promise.

The renewal of the church is always for the
sake of the human community, for which the church
is a sign and foretaste of that kingdom of God
which comes to us both as judgment and as promise

---

3. The Promise of Life in the Kingdom

17. Jesus preaches the kingdom as being like leaven which works until the whole — church, humankind, all of creation — has been leavened (cf. Matt. 13:33). This universal message comes from the Lord "who calls you into his own kingdom and glory" (1 Thess. 2:12). The kingdom, with its judgment, grace, challenge and promise, is thus related to the whole of humanity and to each individual.

18. Through the message of the kingdom the Holy Spirit discloses to the world what sin, justice and *judgment* are (cf. John 16:8-11). Before God, who is just, holy and almighty, sinful humanity is under judgment. Therefore Jesus calls all people to repentance in order that they may turn from a sinful, self-centered life to a life in community in accordance with God's will.

19. At the same time the coming of the kingdom is an event full of *grace* and offered to all human beings. It cannot be earned; it is not the result or fulfilment of human activities. Rather it is a gift of grace beyond full comprehension, a gift which intends to communicate eternal salvation to human beings and which awaits their response of faith.

20. The message of the kingdom is a *challenge* to all humanity. Because it offers a unique opportunity for new life and hope, this message confronts each individual and community with the choice between rejecting the kingdom and making a radical and total decision for it. Such a decision reaches to the roots of existence and includes within its scope all areas of life.

21. The fully accomplished kingdom of God will be a "new heaven and a new earth" (Rev. 21:l). This *promise* includes the gift of radical newness and of all-embracing community: "Behold, I make all things new" (Rev. 21:5). Life under this promise will, already here and now, be a life full of hope. The message of the kingdom is in a special way addressed as hope and promise to the poor, that is, those without power, sufficient material means, a voice in society (Luke 4:18-19; cf. Isa. 61:1-3). Therefore the church is given a particular responsibility both in mission to the poor, and in being called to listen to the voice of the poor as a help in discerning God's liberating activity — that is, the signs of the kingdom. With the presence of the kingdom in the person of Christ the history and destiny of all humanity has undergone a fundamental change. And with the parousia of Jesus Christ there will once again be a radical and comprehensive transformation and fulfilment.

22. The advent of the kingdom of God is God's generous gift. The generosity of God overflows the narrow confines in which humanity tries to contain it; the kingdom of God will come to the just and the unjust, to those who know God and those who do not. But what does life in the kingdom include? St. Paul offers one way of describing it when he writes: "For the kingdom of God is not a matter of eating or drinking, but of justice and peace and joy in the Holy Spirit" (Rom. 14:17).

A. JUSTICE

23. Justice is a rich theme running throughout the Scriptures. The Old Testament view of justice includes the notion of a right relationship both with God and with one's fellow human beings. Within this covenant relationship God is revealed as the liberator of the oppressed and the defender of the poor, demanding from human beings that they act justly toward one another. Jesus Christ interpreted God's law of justice in terms of participating in God's love towards the world; by his actions and teaching, Jesus united in an indivisible way the relationship of human beings to God with their relationship to one another. "Just as you did it to one of the least of these who are members of my family, you did it to me" (Matt. 25:40). Christ proclaimed the intervention of God's justice on behalf of the needy and the oppressed; he gave his life for the salvation and liberation of human beings. The kingdom

of God is a kingdom of justice, in which the oppressed are liberated and human beings live in a loving relationship with God and with others.

24. Human beings are caught in the web of the results of sinful past actions which spoil the present, causing broken relationships, shattered dreams and personal guilt. But it is not only the past which keeps them captive; they also participate in and contribute to situations of brokenness in the present. And the future, too, lays its claim upon them: their present is limited by the fear of death.

> Those who wield power — economic, political, military, social, scientific, cultural, legal, religious — must be stewards of God's justice and peace. In Christ, God's power is demonstrated in redemptive suffering, as compassionate love which identifies itself with broken and suffering humanity. This empowers people to proclaim the message of liberation, love and hope which offers new life, to resist injustice and to struggle against the powers of death.
>
> World Convocation on Justice, Peace
> and the Integrity of Creation, Seoul, 1989

25. Yet God's promises meet human need in all its forms. The "good news" which liberates from captivity to both past and present is the forgiveness of sin and the gift of grace, by which human beings can amend their lives and begin, or continue, to grow in holiness. This holiness is revealed in the person of Jesus Christ.

26. The promise of liberation includes the search for justice. The consultation at Porto Alegre reported:

> The Church as the new people of God is a community of believers determined by the presence of the Kingdom of God in Jesus Christ, and by the twofold commandment to love God above all else, and to love one's neighbor as oneself. The community of believers is challenged especially in the face of the manifold injustices in the world.
>
> Consultation Report, para. 44;
> *Mid-Stream*, XXVIII, 1, pp. 113-114

This dimension will be explored in the discussion of the justice issues in Chapter IV.

B. PEACE

27. There is considerable scriptural witness to the concept of "peace". It can be traced in the prophetic tradition of the Old Testament and throughout the New Testament, in both the gospels and epistles. "Shalom" connotes whole-

ness. It is not merely an absence of conflict, but a state of well-being and harmony in which all relationships are rightly ordered between God, human-kind and creation. Peace is a promise associated with the coming of the kingdom of God; the basis of peace is God's judgment as final arbiter (Isa. 2:3-4.). All other forms of peace, though desirable, are provisional and fragile.

28. The church becomes a sign of the kingdom of God when relationships within the Christian community are characterised by the recognition of the personal value and worth of each human being. Such a community was described at the Prague Consultation as one "where hurting and healing both take place within the circle of God's love and so healing can prevail" (*Beyond Unity-In-Tension*, p. 155). The teaching of the New Testament further under-lines this insight when Christians are asked to "Bear one another's burdens and so fulfil the law of Christ", (Gal. 6:2) or exhorted in this way: "Let each of you look not to your own interests, but to the interests of others" (Phil. 2:4). The promises of the kingdom of God are here characterized by relationships of mutual interdependence, as in a family. But the kingdom of God is not limited to the intimacy of the family and the home; it embraces all the nations of the earth and the boundlessness of the heavens. So the intimate qualities of human relationships within the family are applied to relationships within communities, within and between nations, and with the whole created order.

29. But this world is one of sin and brokenness, a world which does not conform to this vision of peace. This brokenness is pictured already in the account of the Garden of Eden, as God speaks with the serpent, the woman and the man (Gen. 3:14-19). The harmony which had existed earlier between the man and woman, between humankind and the creation, and between human activity and the processes of nature, has now been disrupted. There is no "peace": therefore we pray "forgive us our debts" and "your kingdom come" (Matt. 6:12, 10).

"Shalom"... is not merely an absence of conflict, but a state of well-being and harmony in which all relationships are rightly ordered between God, humankind and creation

---

30. God's judgment in the garden of Eden discloses a disruption in the relationships between humanity and the created order. Today the effects of this disruption have become more and more apparent. One can discern in Scripture the goodness and integrity of creation, both in the account of the origins of the world — "God saw everything that he had made, and indeed, it was very good" (Gen. 1:31) — and in Creation's longing for the final appearance of God's kingdom (cf. Rom. 8:19). Creation has been entrusted to human hands. Careful stewardship is needed to safeguard its limited resour-ces, indeed to ensure its very survival.

31. In an age of global communication, when news of disputes occurring anywhere on the planet can be brought into every home, there is a deep yearning for national and international conflict to be met by the promises of God. The hope of "peace with justice" is one of the great desires of this present age.

32. Christians have a role to play in bringing about such peace. In the baptismal affirmation of Galatians 3:27-28 there is the promise of a community which is one, in which there are no barriers of race, class or sex. The Epistle to the Ephesians speaks of Christ as:

> our peace, who has made us both one, and has broken down the dividing wall of hostility... that he might create in himself one new humanity in place of the two, so making peace, and might reconcile both to God in one body through the cross (Eph. 2:14-16).

In the partial realization of this promise, the church is to be a sign of that eschatological hope of the "breaking down" of barriers which will enable the whole human community to live in peace.

C. JOY IN THE HOLY SPIRIT

33. "Blessed are the poor in spirit, for theirs is the kingdom of heaven" (Matt. 5:3). The unfolding revelation of God's promise of the kingdom in the Scriptures gradually unveils it as one of joy. Proclaiming the future action of

God on behalf of the chosen people, Isaiah speaks words of comfort: "Get you up to a high mountain, O Zion, herald of good tidings; ...say to the cities of Judah, 'Behold your God'" (Isa. 40:9-10). In the New Testament, Jesus' birth is announced by angels as "good news of great joy" (Luke 2:10) and the four accounts of his life, ministry, death and resurrection are called gospels — "good news". Jesus' mission was to proclaim glad tidings to the poor (Luke 4:18); he rejoiced that God's mystery is revealed to the "little ones" (Luke 10:21); he teaches that the repentance of one sinner brings great joy in heaven (Luke 15:7, 10). Jesus' words and deeds show that the path to joy leads through suffering and the cross. In John's gospel are found these words: "So you have pain now, but I will see you again and your hearts will rejoice, and no one will take your joy from you" (John 16:22).

34. One of the powerful symbols Jesus chose to convey his message of the kingdom was table fellowship — the sharing of meals, especially with outcasts and sinners. This activity was matched by the parables in which Jesus taught that the kingdom of heaven is like a joyous wedding banquet (Matt. 22:1-14). The communion of human beings with God and with one another, the communion which Jesus came to establish, received its highest expression in the Lord's Supper. The eucharist is an eschatological feast of joy, a witness that the kingdom has arrived in Jesus Christ and a foretaste of the reign of God which is yet to be.

35. The church as the body of Christ participates in Jesus' mission in the course of history. "While he blessed them, he parted from them. And they returned to Jerusalem with great joy, and they were continually in the temple blessing God" (Luke 24:51-53). The church is a community of joy which continues to proclaim Christ's good news of salvation. It continues to live the Lord's paschal mystery of dying and rising again. From the suffering of his prison cell, Paul could write to the community at Philippi: "Rejoice in the Lord always; again I will say, Rejoice" (Phil. 4:4). The church must continue to be an effective sign to the world that the Lord "who is mighty has done great things for me" (Luke 1:49), that "he has helped his servant Israel" (Luke 1:54).

Questions for Reflection and Discussion

1. In light of the biblical witness how do you understand your own calling as a Christian today?

2. Is the unity of the church an important concern for your Christian community? If so, how does it express this concern?

3. In your experience, how does the overcoming of divisions in and between churches affect the rest of the human community?

CHAPTER III

Kingdom — Church — Humanity

1. In God's creation all human beings are made in the image of God. In the kingdom of God both the church and the whole of humanity have their goal. It is, therefore, in this dimension of their common origin and common goal that the inter-relation of church and humanity in their struggle for renewal and unity can best be understood. This points also to the wider framework of the history of God's saving action, in which the church participates as mystery and prophetic sign, as a communion in and for the world. This chapter explores these dimensions of the reality and life of the church.

1. Ecclesiological Presuppositions

2. The Bible describes the church through a variety of images that denote its relationship to God and the way in which this relationship is actualized and manifested in its life of worship, witness and service. In the church, humanity and the whole creation is united with God in Jesus Christ; and from this perspective the church can be understood as a divine-human reality which both includes and transcends its empirical and historical expressions.

3. The church has been founded, in continuity with the people of God of the Old Covenant and with the preaching of the gospel of Jesus Christ about the coming reign of God, upon the new covenant made with humankind in Christ's blood (1 Cor. 11:25). The centre of the church's life is the risen and reigning Christ, who is its Lord, its head, and the source of its life and mission. He is present and active in it even as it is his body through the power of the Holy Spirit.

4. The church is led by the Spirit into a new relationship with God; this enables it to participate in the life of God (Acts 2:1-21) and makes it a vital communion, the one mystical body of Christ. The whole life of the church should be conceived as a continuous Pentecost through the invocation of the Spirit (*epiclesis*), as it is by the operation of the Holy Spirit that the faithful are sustained and equipped for their life and witness in the world.

> All the baptized are incorporated into one body which is called to witness to its one and only Saviour. Christians are called to manifest the unity they have in Christ by their oneness in the apostolic faith and in the sacramental life...This unity does not imply uniformity, but an organic bond of unity between all the local churches in the richness of their diversities.
>
> *Confessing The One Faith*

5. The faithful as the body of Christ participate in the trinitarian life of communion and love. This makes the church a *koinonia* (community) rooted in and sustained by the communion of Father, Son and the Holy Spirit. It is thus a mystery and a sign pointing to and serving the Triune God's work towards the salvation and renewal of all humankind.

2. Kingdom and Church

6. By preaching the good news, that is, the coming of the kingdom of God, and by the active presence of the kingdom in his life, his passion and his resurrection, Jesus Christ through the Holy Spirit laid the foundations of his church. Whoever receives this message, and is led by the Holy Spirit to affirm it in faith and to be baptized, belongs to Christ's church. The members of the church will not be separated from the rest of humanity, but related to it in a deeper way and committed to it even more strongly. When God, from the human race, calls together the church (*ekklesia*), it is because God wills it to be a sign of the reconciliation of human beings to God and to one another. It not only points to something else, but is already the effective beginning of the new humanity. It unites in this all those who acknowledge the claim of the sovereign reign of God, which itself implies the necessity of constant conversion and renewal in the power of the Holy Spirit.

7. The church is called to be in all aspects oriented towards the final coming of the kingdom of which it is already a foretaste, especially in the Lord's Supper, which is the communion of Christ's eschatological meal with his people. The church anticipates the yet greater blessings which God has in store and which surpass present human experience. That is why the church yearns and prays so fervently: "Your kingdom come" (Matt. 6:10; Luke 11:2), "Maranatha", "Our Lord, come!" (1 Cor. 16:22), "And the Spirit and the bride say, 'Come'" (Rev. 22:17).

8. The church is that part of humanity which has been led to accept, affirm and acknowledge ever more fully the liberating truth of the kingdom for all people. It is the community of those who are experiencing the presence of the kingdom and actively awaiting its final fulfilment. The church is therefore called to live as that force within humanity through which God's will for the renewal, justice, community and salvation of all people is witnessed to.

Endowed with the gifts of the Holy Spirit and continually strengthened by Christ's word and sacrament, the church is sent by God to witness to, and proclaim the kingdom in and for, this broken world through word and deed, life and suffering, even suffering unto death. In this mission the church is the new community of those willing to serve the kingdom for the glory of God and the good of humanity. To the degree to which this happens the church is an effective sign, an instrument of God's mission in this aeon (*aion*).

9. In all this the church participates in the paradoxes and dynamic of the kingdom within history. It, too, is a net with good and bad fish, a field of wheat and tares. It is a community of sinners and at the same time justified, a beginning not an end, always endangered from within as from without, but preserved at the same time by the grace of God in an unendingly renewing feast of Pentecost.

3. Church and Humanity

10. It is in and for the world that God calls the church to be the people of God, a servant-people, the living temple of the Holy Spirit, the bride and body of God's Son, Jesus Christ, in order that it may be a sign and bearer of the Triune God's work towards the salvation and renewal of all humankind. For the fulfilment of this vocation God wills the churches to move toward that unity for which Jesus prayed, a unity visible to the world and having a spiritual authenticity as a communion of worship, witness and service which can help the world to respond to God in faith (cf. Matt. 5:16, "Let your light shine before others..."; cf. in the present text Chapter I, para. 5).

11. This call of God comes to the church in a world marked by the broken relationship between creator and creature which is a consequence of human sin and has as its consequence brokenness within all of creation, including humanity and history. The historical fragmentation and the tensions and conflicts within Christianity are also part of, and sometimes contribute to, the brokenness of the world. Thus the church in its life and mission experiences, as did its Head and Lord, the consequences of cosmic brokenness. This is its suffering and struggle. The church's hope resides in the fact that God, for his part, has never let go of the world nor given up his saving design for it.

...despite the scandal of our divisions, we may together mend our ways and bear witness to the world that the reign of peace and justice is already in the midst of us... A Church which only spoke of economics or ecology would soon become insignificant for the experts in these fields can always surpass it. Our far more serious responsibility is to test day by day the evangelical quality of our existence.

Cardinal Roger Etchegaray, "Peace with Justice..."

12. In their reaction against brokenness and in their search for wholeness, many people and nations strive for unity on the basis of the aspirations and common humanity which God has given to them. What should distinguish the churches' reaction against brokenness, and their striving for visible unity, is God's forgiveness accomplished in Christ and the unity already given by Christ. Such unity is already experienced in the communion shared by Christians. It is the basis for renewal and reconciliation among them and enables their common witness and service.

13. In the perspective of the kingdom of God it becomes possible to speak about the relation between church and world without one-sided distortion. This perspective implies, first of all, that the relation between church and world depends ultimately on a final act of God in which God's promise of redemption becomes full reality. In this way any premature amalgamation and confusion between church and world is precluded. There is, in other words, a legitimate concern for the inalienable identity of the church as distinct from the world, in the church's intrinsic relation to God the Father, Son and Holy Spirit, while at the same time the relationship between church and world is recognized and practised in hope.

14. The perspective of the kingdom implies, secondly, that the church can be truly recognized as consisting of the "stuff" of the world, even as it is not "of" the world (cf. John 15:19). What is gathered, reconciled and renewed in the church is, in fact, "world" in its estrangement from God and therefore this renewing process continually refers back to the world and forward to its final redemption.

15. There are also many forces of renewal active in the world which can be seen, through the eyes of faith, as expressions of God's continuing care for creation. Recognizing these the church is called to its own proper responsibility and mission; when true to itself and guided by its Lord, "the Church can go out to the edges of society, not fearful of being distorted or confused by the world's agenda, but confident and capable of recognizing that God is already there at work" (*Gathered for Life*, p. 50). As the church witnesses to the final fulfilment, which is also the world's future, it bears the world's problems within itself in solidarity and in hope.

4. The Church as Mystery

16. Many images for the church exist already in the New Testament, and there has been a long history of reflection upon them. In its effort to describe the place of the church in God's design and work for the renewal and salvation of humanity, the Unity and Renewal study has found the concepts of *mystery* and of *sign* particularly helpful. Both have been and are used by several Christian traditions in their efforts to express fundamental truths about the church. The term "mystery" indicates a basic insight which Christians already have in common, namely the admission of their inability to speak adequately about the church. By "mystery" the Bible points to a reality which transcends human comprehension and, even more so, human pos-

sibilities of expression, a reality which becomes evident only in the degree to which God wills and accomplishes it.

17. In the New Testament the word "mystery" designates God's primal intention to accomplish the salvation of all humanity through Jesus Christ: "For he has made known to us in all wisdom and insight the mystery of his will, according to his purpose which he set forth in Christ as a plan for the fullness of time, to unite all things in him, things in heaven and things on earth" (Eph. 1:9-10; cf. Col. 1:15-20). The church belongs in its essence to this saving event. Thus, when the word "mystery" is applied to the church, it refers to the church as a reality which transcends its empirical, historical expression — a reality which is rooted in, and sustained and shaped by, the communion of Father, Son and Holy Spirit. Therefore with "mystery" the accent will fall on that saving communion with Christ which the church already enjoys in faith and upon whose final scope no limits are set; it will be a question of the eventual inclusion of the whole world in the kingdom already known to the church.

... when the word "mystery" is applied to the church,
it refers to the church as a reality which transcends
its empirical, historical expression — a reality
which is rooted in, and sustained and shaped by, the
communion of Father, Son and Holy Spirit

---

18. This mystery is revealed to faith by the Holy Spirit who knows the deep things of God (1 Cor. 2:7-10). Although in the New Testament the church is not explicitly called "mystery", Ephesians uses the word "mystery" to indicate the close communion between Christ and the church (Eph. 5:32). The mystery of "Christ in you" is for believers their "hope of glory" (Col. 1:27). The function of Christian preaching is to "declare the mystery of Christ" (Col. 4:3; cf. Eph.3:7-11). The mystery "will be fulfilled" at the last trumpet (Rev. 10:7; cf. 1 Cor. 15:51-55).

19. The mystery of the divine-human relationship revealed in Jesus Christ is therefore the foundation of unity and community for God's people. In Ephesians Paul speaks of his insight into the "mystery of Christ" who is our peace, breaking down the dividing wall of hostility, reconciling separated peoples in one body through the Cross (Eph. 2:14-16, 3:4-6). The incarnation is an invitation to share in the glorified humanity of Christ, to be renewed in the image of God and to share in the suffering of Christ for the world.

20. On the day of Pentecost the Holy Spirit brought the followers of Christ into a new relationship to God by imparting a share in the life of God (Acts 2:1-21). In that same pentecostal act each believer is brought into a new relation with other believers, forming a vital communion, the one mystical

body of Christ. They are gathered in the church, which is sent into the world in order to be a foretaste of what the world is to become, the firstfruits of the new creation.

21. As the body of Christ, the church participates in the divine mystery. As mystery, it reveals Christ to the world by proclaiming the gospel, by celebrating the sacraments (which are themselves called "mysteries"), and by manifesting the newness of life given by him, thus anticipating the kingdom already present in him.

> The struggle for justice is both an essential part of the mystery of the church and a means for experiencing more deeply this mystery, that is, the self-disclosure and self-giving presence of the Triune God in the Incarnate Son, realized ever anew by the Holy Spirit.
>
> Porto Alegre Consultation Report, para. 43, No. 6;
> *Mid-Stream*, XXVIII, 1, p. 113

The church is united with Christ in the humiliation of the Cross while at the same time it experiences the victory of the resurrection, thus making present in the life of this world the new life of the kingdom — present now, yet still to come.

22. The core of this life in Christ embraces historical and natural reality so that the church is intimately related to the whole of creation. The new creation (*kaine ktisis*) will unite the whole of the created order with God's love and purpose for its continuing renewal and perfection in Christ (2 Cor. 5:17; Col. 1:16f.). However, the new creation is not yet completed. The church therefore stands with creation in anticipation of renewal, groaning in travail, waiting for final redemption (Rom. 8:21-22).

23. The term "mystery" and the term "sign", which will be introduced in the next section, should be seen as closely inter-related and complementary. The mystery of God's presence in the church is already a sign addressed to the world. And the church as sign is an invitation to the world to let itself be permeated by the divine mystery. These two ecclesiological perspectives are always in tension with the reality of the church as a historical, human community. This tension cannot be solved by separating the "divine nature" of the church from its "human nature." Rather, this tension is the deepest challenge to a constant renewal of the life of the church in order that it may better correspond to its divine calling and mission as mystery and sign for the world.

5. The Church as Prophetic Sign

24. Another term which is helpful in expressing the relationship between church and humanity in the perspective of the kingdom of God is the term "sign".

25. The word "sign" can make clear that the church is there for others. It must point not to itself but beyond itself. Its character as sign derives not from itself but from its Lord. The concept of sign indicates especially the essential relation between church and world. Called by God out of the world the church is placed in the world's service; it is destined to be God's sign for the world by proclaiming the gospel and living a life of loving service to humanity. It is thus God's pointer to what God wants to tell the world and to give to it. Thus the church is called constantly to look both to its Lord, to whom it owes all, and to humanity, to which it is fully committed. If the

adjective "prophetic" is attached to the term "sign", it is in order to recall the dimensions of judgment and salvation, and the eschatological perspective which inheres to the notion of mystery and is often implied in the biblical occurrences of "sign".

A. Sign: biblical foundation

26. The term "sign" is used frequently in the Scriptures. But this usage carries different and diverse meanings. For example, "sign" can indicate an effective reality (the sign signifies what is effected), or a sign is understood in a "symbolical" sense (it refers to another reality); and there can also be an overlapping of these two meanings according to the specific context. In this text "sign" is used in the sense of something pointing beyond itself and at the same time participating in that to which it points. In the following paragraphs only some instances of the wide and diverse use of "sign" in the Bible are given.

27. For example, in the Old Testament God sometimes through signs reveals directly to the people of Israel his purposes in creation (the sun and moon as indicators of times and seasons, Gen. 1:14) and covenant (the rainbow as sign of the covenant with every living creature and all future generations, Gen. 9:12-17). Signs given through the prophets are an acting out of the divine message by the prophets themselves in relation to contemporary events (for example Jer. 27, Hos. 3 and Habakkuk). Of special importance for these reflections is that the covenant people of Israel itself may serve as God's "ensign" (signal) to the nations as in Isaiah 49:22 (cf. also Isa. 8:18).

28. In the New Testament, particularly in the fourth gospel, the miraculous deeds of Jesus are termed "signs" (*semeia*) (John 2:11, 3:2, 4:54, 6:2, 12:18, 20:30; cf. Acts 2:22). These designate Jesus as the one who has come from God and to whom attention must be given (John 3:2). In his teaching Jesus strongly resists the demands of "an evil and adulterous generation" for signs, in the sense of miracles that would "prove" that Jesus spoke the truth but were unconnected with the substantive content of his message. The "sign" this generation will receive is the "sign of Jonah": a prophetic prefiguration of Christ's death and resurrection, and of the repentance of the Gentiles (Matt. 12:38-42).

29. In the context of the feeding of the multitude (John 6:25ff.), the people again see a "sign", comparable in this case to the giving of the manna in the wilderness. Jesus makes clear that the true "bread from heaven" is himself, given by God for the life of the world. God's people participate in this "sign" as they participate in the "sign" performed by Jesus at the marriage feast of Cana (John 2:1-11). Both signs appeal to the response of faith and point forward to the transforming of creation and the rejoicing of God's people at the fulfilment in God's kingdom (see Isa. 55:12-13).

30. The "signs" of Jesus do not end with his earthly life. Indeed, references to *semeia* which the apostles carry out in the name of Jesus are found already in the early chapters of the Acts of the Apostles (2:43, 4:30, 6:8, 14:3; cf. 2 Cor. 12:12). At the Jerusalem Council, Barnabas and Paul appeal to these signs as evidence that God wills the inclusion of Gentiles in the Christian community. Thus these texts broaden the original scope of the term, and hence prepare the way for thinking of the church itself as a sign.

31. The "sign" present in Jesus is visible, however, only to the eyes of faith. And in light of the diverse uses of the term "sign", all talk of the church as "sign" is possible only if it is directly connected with the "mystery" of Christ, the "mystery revealed" (cf. Col. 1:26-27) of God's saving purpose to unite all things and people in Christ through the preaching of the gospel and the response to it (cf. Eph. 1:10, 3:5). It is Christ, present and active in the church through the Holy Spirit, who makes the church through its life, witness and service a sign of judgment and salvation to all humankind. Thus the church is a sign pointing beyond itself to Christ, with whom it is at the same time intimately united as his body. The church is also a sign pointing beyond itself to the kingdom of God, to which, in God's purpose, it is at the same time united as its firstfruit.

B. PROPHETIC MINISTRY AND SIGN

32. Christians are called to exercise within the church a dynamic prophetic ministry as a vital part of the general task of preaching and living the gospel. Within that community this prophetic ministry seeks to relate the gospel to the critical events and issues of the day. The church itself may first need to hear a prophetic word, but such a prophetic ministry is not individualistic: it is to be tested by the community of faith and is also a responsibility of that community, one which it exercises by bearing witness to both the judgment and the promise of the kingdom. Not every event or issue is the subject of direct references in the Scriptures; some of them lead Christians who are involved in them to fresh insights from the witness of Scripture and Tradition for their time. Thus the church's prophetic ministry, both within its own life and to the world, is challenged and informed by contemporary events and causes.

> In its function as "sign" the African-American church points to injustice and unrighteousness existing within both the church as 'people of God' and the world. As a sign, it has stressed the importance of struggle and redemptive suffering in the process of reconciliation...
>
> Harlem Consultation Report, p. 6;
> *Mid-Stream*, XXVIII, 4, p. 417

33. It is in relation to this mutual challenging of world and church that — in addition to the concept of the church as sign — signs may be recognized in the world and in the church, signs which are there in order that they may be read and understood (cf. Hab. 2:2) in the light of God's revelation in Jesus Christ and related to the all-encompassing plan of salvation of the Triune God. This requires of the church, in its vocation to be a prophetic sign pointing to God's judgment and salvation in Jesus Christ, a double implementation of its witnessing task, an implementation both in the communication of God's truth and in the sharing of God's love.

C. COMMUNICATING GOD'S TRUTH FOR FAITH

34. In word and sacraments and common life the church is called to communicate by "translating" (in a more than linguistic sense: that is, by "incarnating") the gospel message intended for all humankind so that it may be heard, understood and accepted in all cultures. The church communicates and translates the gospel from within one culture to another; it cannot avoid becoming involved with the particularities of each culture. These particularities must themselves be open to change as the Gospel is handed on. The church, by its universal nature, is to be located within all cultures as well as being sent to all cultures. It is both concretely local and truly catholic. This is one aspect of the continuing Pentecost in the life of the church, as the Holy Spirit enables the church to become an intelligible and effective prophetic

sign to people in all cultures, summoning them to unity in Christ through repentance and faith.

35. Through Pentecost Christians begin to reverse the confusion of Babel: they begin to learn how to communicate and apply the universal gospel across, and to, the variety and division of issues and cultures. In this living tradition of handing on and communicating the gospel as an expression of the process of Pentecost, the prophetic witness of the church points towards the coming of Christ in glory and the fulfilment of God's plan of salvation. In this twofold perspective the church is a prophetic sign pointing to the catholic as well as eschatological dimension of God's life-giving truth.

The Church is local when the saving event of Christ takes root in a particular local situation with all its natural, social, cultural and other characteristics which make up the life and thought of the people living in that place. Just as it happens in the Eucharist where the people offer to God as the Body of Christ all that is "his own" (the fruits of the earth together with the products of their everyday labour), the same must apply to the Church's life, if it is to be truly local: it must absorb and use all the characteristics of a given local situation and not impose an alien culture on it.

John Zizioulas, "The Local Church..."

---

36. The handing on of God's truth must be grounded in faithfulness to the apostolic faith of the church. Such faithfulness, in the context of contemporary situations and events, will encounter opposition and controversy, and therefore involves taking risks and seeking to speak a painful truth in love. Prophetic ministry, however, must be tested by criteria. Faithfulness to the apostolic faith, self-criticism of efforts to communicate the gospel, and creative application of the gospel to contemporary issues and situations are all necessary to the Christian's prophetic ministry. Faithfulness without self-criticism and creative application would offer only a "dead letter". Self-criticism without faithfulness and creative application would prevent any convincing communication of the gospel. Creative application without faithfulness and self-criticism would produce only a spurious "relevance".

37. By serving as a prophetic sign through the communication and application of God's truth to concrete situations in all cultures and conditions in the world, the church is itself renewed and serves at the same time the renewal of human community. The handing on of God's truth in its many-sided nature, while it often produces tension, can become a reconciling communication.

D. THE SHARING OF GOD'S LOVE IN CHRIST

38. In offering its common life in the service of God and God's love for the world, the church has also constantly to struggle both through its presence

alongside those who suffer and by its action on their behalf. In this sharing of God's love the church enables them to perceive the suffering love of God in Jesus Christ for them, and the church itself is led to a deeper experience of that love.

39. In thus giving a share of God's love through involvement in the world, the church is a sign of the presence of the kingdom of God in Jesus Christ. Therefore its struggle is something quite other than mere activism, and a prophetic church may meet with the painful rejection which the biblical prophets often encountered. Furthermore, the "sign" should not become the centre of attention in its own right. Much Christian self-understanding is distorted by self-centredness, and there is always a danger that teaching concerning the church itself will be misunderstood in this manner. The church should be centred upon Christ and upon God's purpose of salvation. Those who are sent to be a prophetic sign of God's purpose and love in the world and who are "called, beloved in God the Father and kept for Jesus Christ" must also "keep" themselves "in the love of God" (Jude 1, 21).

40. It is in relation to the double task of communicating God's truth and of sharing God's love described above that it is possible to see the relationship between cross and resurrection in the life of the church. We carry "in the body the death of Jesus, so that the life of Jesus may also be made visible in our bodies" (2 Cor. 4:10). A church whose glory is the glory of the crucified and risen Lord will become a sign by its involvement in the world's divisions and sufferings for the sake of their being overcome by Christ. It will not be a self-protective, aloof body but a ferment, a seed, the first-fruits of harvest. The church's self-emptying will make it transparent to the one who, though he is rich, yet for the sake of others became poor, so that they might be filled with the riches of God.

...the church is a sign of the presence of the kingdom of God in Jesus Christ... its struggle is something quite other than mere activism, and a prophetic church may meet with the painful rejection which the biblical prophets often encountered

---

E. THE HOLY SPIRIT, UNITY AND RENEWAL

41. The church is a community called to manifest and signify, in a specific way and through a chosen group, the permanence of God's personal relationship with the whole creation, a relationship sustained by the Holy Spirit. The human struggles "outside" the church for justice, peace, care of the earth, liberation and true partnership between men and women are not elements foreign to the one creation of God. They call for Christian solidarity. Therefore the church's witness, which is guided and filled by the Holy Spirit, includes the judgment of the whole world (John 16:8-11), a share in its

suffering (John 15:20), and a manifestation, in the world, of renewal in the form of reconciliation and new life (John 11:24-25).

42. God the Father glorifies the Son as by death and resurrection the way is opened to new life in the Spirit. It is by this continuing Pentecost that the church is united and renewed in the love of the Holy Trinity to find a life in unity. So renewed and so moving towards visible unity, the church is both a sign and a means of renewal in the human community, a renewal which can only find its authenticity and fullness as humankind is drawn together towards the consummation of God's creation in the perfected kingdom.

6. Dimensions of the Mission of the Church

43. In speaking of the church as mystery and prophetic sign this chapter has presented an understanding of the church in its worshipping communion, witness and service for the renewal of human community, and sought to show how the church's mission is an integral dimension of its nature. This concluding section, therefore, does not add a further element or function of the church but explicates what has already been said.

A. THE CHURCH AS COMMUNION IN AND FOR THE WORLD

44. In recent ecumenical discussions and within several churches the understanding of the church as *koinonia* (embracing the themes of community, communion, participation) has found increased attention and acceptance. It embraces "mystery", "prophetic sign" and other images and terms for the church. Accordingly, *koinonia* also implies the indissoluble inter-relation between the nature and the mission of the church.

Led by the reconciling love of God, strengthened
by the mystery of its sacramental life in Christ,
and informed by prophetic judgment, the church
is called to serve humanity in the struggle for
renewal and transformation.

---

45. Through the proclamation of the Word of God and the celebration of the sacraments the church is constantly assembled and strengthened by the Holy Spirit as a community or communion *(koinonia)*. It participates in the communion of the Holy Trinity and is thereby in communion with the saints of all ages and places. Each local Christian community receives the gift of reconciliation and renewed life within itself, and is called to be in communion with all other local Christian communities. As a reconciled, renewed community it is sent to live and witness as a sign and instrument of reconciliation and renewal in the world.

46. The life of the church celebrates and communicates this renewal and reconciliation. By taking elements from creation and celebrating their being used and sanctified by God to convey the saving presence of God through word and sacraments, the church witnesses to the restored relation between God and the cosmos as the new creation in Christ. The sanctifying work of the Holy Spirit in the preaching, sacraments and life of the church is an authentic and evangelical demonstration of the unity and renewal which is already experienced in faith, and to which the world is destined.

47. Through the church as living communion God manifests saving and uniting grace to all creation. In its eucharistic communion Christ is the source and goal of the unity of the church and of the renewal of human community.

> As Jesus went out to publicans and sinners and had table-fellowship with them during his earthly ministry, so Christians are called in the eucharist to be in solidarity with the outcast and to become signs of the love of Christ who lived and sacrificed himself for all and now gives himself in the eucharist.
>
> *Baptism, Eucharist and Ministry*, Eucharist, para. 24

Washed and liberated by Christ's suffering the witness of Christians takes the form of suffering with the world and for the world. Filled with hope by Christ's victory over death in his resurrection, their witness takes the form of joyous and confident affirmation of God's reconciling and saving purpose for the world.

48. Participating in such communion with Christ calls believers to repentance, renewed commitment and solidarity with those who seek fully human existence in the church and the world. Led by the reconciling love of God, strengthened by the mystery of its sacramental life in Christ, and informed by prophetic judgment, the church is called to serve humanity in the struggle for renewal and transformation.

> It is the church that should give the lead for the relationship of men and women in society. The church is the sign of the coming unity and a paradigm for society's living. Our dream is for a community where men and women live in complementarity and share life and joy.
>
> Benin Consultation Report, p. 9

49. The church as mystery and prophetic sign, a communion sustained by the Holy Spirit, is sent by God to continue the mission of Christ, in whom the kingdom of God became present among us as a life-giving reality to be offered to all. This mission of the church is at the same time grounded in its character as a sign pointing to, and participating in, God's saving and reconciling action for all of humanity.

50. In the unity which is God's gift and in their struggle to manifest that unity (*oneness*), the churches within the ecumenical movement are called to contribute to the efforts towards unity and reconciliation within the human community, while respecting the great cultural diversity in the contemporary world. God's gift of sanctification (*holiness*) provides spiritual strength to resist the temptation to resignation and conformism and to confront injustice, oppression and alienation in the name of the one who is holy. The church, as the body of Christ by word and sacraments, brings people from all nations and backgrounds into communion in Christ through the Holy Spirit; in its historical reality the church must seek to embrace, in the fullness of one faith, the diversity of local churches with their rites and traditions (*catholicity*). As was said at the Singapore Consultation:

> In such a church, if it is to be truly catholic, there must be room for diversity which welcomes and celebrates the specific gifts of women as well as of men; of young and old; of disabled and marginalized, of ordained and lay, embracing people from different cultures, races and ethnic and social groups.
>   Consultation Report, p. 16; *Mid-Stream*, XXVIII, 1, p. 101

In continuing in the faith and mission of the apostles (*apostolicity*), Christians and their communities are equipped to become witnesses to God's love and grace for all human beings.

B. THE CALLING OF THE CHURCH TO WORSHIP, WITNESS AND SERVICE

51. *Worship*. When the church listens and responds to God's revelation it receives and affirms in the Holy Spirit Christ's message of the kingdom of God. On behalf of all creatures, the church renders praise and thanks to God for God's grace and the forgiveness of sins which it effects. In intercession the gift of that grace for all spheres of life is sought. God's presence and action in the liturgy of the Christian communion enables and sends Christians into the world as witnesses and servants of God for the renewal of human community.

52. *Witness*. As the risen Lord commissioned his disciples to go into the world as witnesses (Acts 1:8) and as teachers (Matt. 28:16-20), so God continues to call and send the church to point in all times and places to him who is uniquely "the way, and the truth, and the life" (John 14:6). All members of the *koinonia* are called to render this witness through a variety of gifts and in the manifold situations in which they live. This witness finds expression in worship, in common witness of Christians from different churches, in evangelisation, in commitment to social change, in dialogue with people of other living faiths, in advocating the cause of those who cannot yet speak for themselves, and in enabling the voiceless to speak.

53. Such witness may lead to the suffering of Christians, including that of the multitude of known and unknown martyrs of all times and in many parts of the world today.

There is also redemptive suffering for which one assumes the posture of the cross, taking on the role of "no power" as did Dr. Martin Luther King, Jr. Suffering which comes in an effort to bring justice for others is mysterious; yet it can be redemptive.

Harlem Consultation Report, p. 4;
Mid-Stream, XXVIII, 4, p. 415

But even when such suffering seems to be in vain, the church is sustained by God's faithfulness and by the confident expectation of that day when "every knee shall bow... and every tongue confess that Jesus Christ is Lord" (Phil. 2:10-11).

54. *Service*. As the early church responded to the grace of God with worship and witness, it also responded with specific acts of service (Acts 6:1-6). Receiving God's love, the church is called to impart this love in service to all humankind in its needs, divisions, sufferings and hopes. Through this service the church as mystery, grounded in the love of the Triune God, becomes a sign of the presence of the kingdom of God in Jesus Christ.

55. In the calling of the church to mission it is clear that worship, witness and service are inter-related and strengthen each other. Worship without witness and service is in danger of becoming separated from the world in which the worshippers live. Service without worship and witness is in danger of becoming purely secular "social action". Witness without worship is in danger of not listening to God's word before speaking. And witness without service is in danger of not seeing human beings in light of their full spiritual and material needs.

56. The church has been evangelized by God, and thus participating in the revealed mystery of God in Christ enters into the divine mission of evangelizing the world by proclaiming the good news of the kingdom. The church has been reconciled to God, and thus becoming a prophetic sign receives from God the ministry of reconciliation within humanity. The church has been gathered by God, and thus living as a Spirit-filled communion in Christ is commissioned to share in the gathering of all God's scattered children.

Questions for Reflection and Discussion

1. What in this chapter's description of the church do you find most helpful? Are there points you would wish to add or to change?

2. How do you experience the inter-relationship between worship, witness, and service in your congregation? How does this relate to or affect its mission?

CHAPTER IV

Unity and Renewal and the Search for Justice

1. The Search for Justice and Christian Unity

1. The church as both mystery and prophetic sign is, according to its divine calling, the firstfruits of the renewed human community made possible by the action of the Triune God. The "mystery" is the now-open, yet still transcendent, secret of God's purpose for salvation, "that through the church the manifold wisdom of God might now be made known to the principalities and powers in the heavenly places" (Eph. 3:10). This cosmic vision is "earthed" in particular places and times and, as was emphatically pointed out in the Harlem consultation with Black Churches in the United States, the mystery has been obscured by the divisive and oppressive actions of fellow Christians who have betrayed their calling. Yet in Christ it has been decisively disclosed in order to lead humankind into a renewed community; and in so far as the Christian community displays God's justice in its life and witness it is a "prophetic sign". This chapter focusses on the implications of the church's contribution to this renewal through its work for justice.

2. Christians live in societies which have various and conflicting understandings of justice. All too often the concept of justice is based upon an ideology and is used to maintain those who have power in power, to maintain the status quo. Even when it is argued that justice is based upon "natural rights" — the individual's freedom to conduct his or her personal affairs, the right to own property, and the right to work — these are, in their turn, seen to depend upon the social structure of the society in which one lives and the prevailing understanding of what it means to be a human being. Such standards of justice may be at variance with the calling of the church to live out God's justice, which has been revealed and handed on to us through Scripture and Christian Tradition.

3. Christians have lived, and in some places still live, in societies in which the understanding of God's justice has informed and permeated the institutions and life of the nation. Many Christians no longer experience such a "Constantinian" situation; they live rather in societies in which there are a multiplicity

of values. This pluralism can confront the church with principles of justice opposed and antagonistic to those which it has received; this confrontation everywhere requires fresh thinking from Christians.

4. In some cases Christians themselves differ about the principles of justice. One Christian community may believe with the Acts of the Apostles that they should have "all things in common" (2:44), but another community may believe in the right to own private property (though such rights are tempered with responsibilities for the welfare of others). But even when agreement is held upon a principle of justice — the sanctity of human life — there are disagreements as to how such principles are applied. One community may believe that abortion is wrong and to be avoided in every circumstance, while another community may believe that it would be right under certain circumstances to procure an abortion, though with sadness. In one community the vocation to pacifism may be be paramount while in another it is considered right, under certain specified circumstances, for one nation to declare war on another.

Where churches are involved in common witness
and joint action in matters of justice this should have
implications for the communion of these
churches with each other

---

5. Christians often remain blind to the injustices which mar human relationships and cannot see that basic structures of their own societies need to be altered. But Christian involvement in the search for more just structures and conditions of human life is clearly called for, and should be seen in close relation to the Christian understanding of the church and its unity. Where churches are involved in common witness and joint action in matters of justice this should have implications for the communion of these churches with each other. Furthermore, churches may have moved closer to each other on their way towards visible unity by resolving those differences of faith and order which have caused denominational separation, yet remain divided, in their living out of the faith and their ordering of church life, by racism, rivalries between social classes or economic groups, or other forms of human brokenness. Such "unity" is not yet the visible unity to which Christians are called by their being one in Christ. Visible unity and the struggle for justice are closely related, as was said in the Fifth International Consultation of United and Uniting Churches at Potsdam:

> The quest for visible unity is related, and must be seen to be
> related, to the overcoming of human divisions and the meeting of
> human needs. This does not mean that the unity of the church is
> only functional, it is also a direct reflection of God's own unity and
> unitive love. Relating unity to mission, service and sharing the

sufferings of humankind is precisely an expression of the love of
God which calls the church into being, as the sign, foretaste and
instrument of a new humanity in the kingdom of God.

Consultation Report, para. 8;
Living Today Towards Visible Unity, p. 6

6. Thus, justice and unity — and with them renewal of the life of the church
and of the human community — belong together. But despite the acknow-
ledgment of this interconnection, justice (on any understanding of it),
renewal and unity are, finally, not achieved by human endeavour. This
ambiguity of the human situation must be recognised by Christians as they
listen to Scripture and Tradition affirming that only God's righteousness,
God's justice (*dikaiosyne*) for all humankind can be the means for salvation and
fulfilment; only God's righteousness, communicated in the saving work of
Christ, is the adequate vision and goal for the human quest.

2. The Understanding of Justice within the Tradition

7. The members of Christ's church understand justice from God's relationship with his people as it is found in Scripture and Tradition — the story of a
just God's dealing with his people. The story begins with a covenant relationship between the Israelites and the God of justice, and this, together with
their own experience of injustice and oppression, not least while they were in
Egypt, provoked a search for the true nature and faithful practice of justice.
Justice came to mean goodness as right relationships. The Christian tradition,
which inherited much of the understanding and experience of the old
covenant, emphasized the personal relationship of the individual with God
and one's neighbour (though the social and communal aspects were not
forgotten). Twentieth century Christians have re-emphasised the social and
communal aspects and have also re-discovered that right relationships
include the place and value of the natural environment in the understanding
and practice of justice.

8. Thus justice is not only about giving each person his or her due, but rather
the restoration of right relationships. In fact God's justice is a vindication of
the poor, the widow, the stranger and all who are oppressed. So justice is
much more than doing works of charity. It can be seen from the biblical
witness that the structures of justice are frequently and easily perverted by
human sinfulness and need to be restored to their integrity as part of God's
design and as pointers to the fulfilment of God's creative and saving work.
There are a number of symbols used in the tradition, including the concepts
of the Jubilee (Lev. 25:8-17, 23-55), the Sabbath (Gen. 2:1-3), the "Rest" of
the people of God (Heb. 4:9-11), the Messianic hope, and the coming of the
kingdom of God (Mark 1:14; cf. Matt. 11:2-6, Luke 7:18-23). Each in its way
has contributed to the Christian understanding of the nature of justice.

9. The traditions embodied in the Old Covenant have been renewed and
enlarged with the coming of Christ. Jesus in his dealings with Zacchaeus

provides a particular model for understanding the concept of justice and love. Jesus goes beyond justice and mercy by stopping in the street and publically demonstrating his friendship and respect: "Zacchaeus, hurry and come down; for I must stay at your house today" (Luke 19:5). It is an outrageous action: Jesus is willing to enter this despicable man's house. Here is a love and a faith in persons that risks failure and rejection in order to try to establish justice. In this instance love *does* establish justice, for Zacchaeus has the courage to give half his possessions to charity and to offer fourfold restitution to anyone he has defrauded.

10. In the life, ministry, death and resurrection of Jesus of Nazareth the message of the Zacchaeus story is universalized and perfected, so that the church has begun to understand that love surpasses justice in the hope that justice can at last be established. In other words there is a connection between God's justification of sinners by grace and the involvement of Christians in the effective working of human systems of justice. "Jesus came into Galilee preaching the gospel of God, and saying 'The time is fulfilled, and the kingdom of God is at hand; repent, and believe in the gospel'" (Mark 1:15). Thus from the opening section of St. Mark's gospel onwards the reader is made aware that the gospel proclamation of the kingdom of God humbles all human pretensions and at the same time kindles human hope. Another biblical aspect of the divine calling to the search for justice is expressed in the words about the kingdom in the Sermon on the Mount, as in Matthew 6:33: "Seek first God's kingdom and God's righteousness, and all these things shall be yours as well". The kingly rule of God lays its demands upon all human situations and upon each situation in a particular way; and for each situation there is good news of God's way of salvation and renewal.

11. The biblical witness about justice leads us to affirm that, in this broken and sinful world, "signs" of justice are ultimately all that Christians can expect. It is a justice which comes from the balancing of claims and interests and the restraint of the actions of sinful human beings. This form of justice must be constantly measured against the divine justice and love which is known in Jesus Christ, and the Christian experience of justification.

Do you really wish to pay homage to Christ's body? Then do not neglect him when he is naked. At the same time that you honor him [in church] with hangings made of silk, do not ignore him outside when he perishes from cold and nakedness... For the One who said "This is my body"... also said "When I was hungry you gave me nothing to eat"...don't neglect your brother in his distress while you decorate Christ's house. Your brother is more truly Christ's temple than any church building.

John Chrysostom, "Homily on Matthew"

---

12. If the church is to be faithful to its calling it will need, as a community of shared faith, to exhibit God's justice in its own corporate life. There is a sense in which the corporate life of the church will involve Christians in witnessing to the world the truth of God's justice. Christians will, however, be aware that there will always be a provisionalty about their witness to and working out of the justice of God within the church. This is because the church lives in the "between times" in which the foretaste of the kingdom of God is given and experienced, but Christians await, as a community of expectation, the completion of God's redeeming work in the final and complete realization of the

kingdom of God. There will, therefore, be a place for judgment and renewal in the justice which the church practises and about which it witnesses.

3. The Universal and the Particular

13. The scriptural understanding of divine righteousness engages Christians with the particular demands arising in each situation. Christians become aware that the search for justice is both a divine calling (what God's will requires) and a human endeavour (what people yearn and struggle for in pursuit of their ideals). Those who are set right by God are impelled to serve their neighbours; one way of such service is the endeavour to secure the neighbour's rights and to establish a basis for the fair distribution of all goods and privileges, with respect for the freedom, dignity and integrity of all persons, "to do justice and to love kindness and to walk humbly with God" (Micah 6:8).

Do you think that someone is a Christian who nourishes no needy person with his bread, who refreshes no thirsty person with his wine, whose table no one shares, under whose roof no stranger or wayfarer abides, whose garments clothe no naked person, whose helping hand assists no pauper... whose mercy no one feels... Far be such an attitude from the minds of all Christians, far be it that any person of this sort be termed a Christian, far be it that such a one should be called the child of God.

St. Augustine, Sermon "On the Christian Life"

---

14. The various forms of contemporary witness making visible the church's given unity, and seeking justice in specific contexts at this particular time in history, must be related to Scripture and to the Tradition of the church through the centuries. The particular is related to the universal across time as well as space.

15. Since every hearing of God's word is a hearing within a particular context the question must always be asked, "What message is being conveyed in this time and place?" The life and witness of the local church is inspired and empowered by hearing such a word, but the local church is impoverished without the support of the whole church and the inspiration of the witness of the church through the ages. This support and inspiration open up new possibilities.

16. Learning from Scripture and Tradition (cf. the insights contained in *The Fourth World Conference on Faith and Order: The Report from Montreal 1963*, pp. 50-61) in particular contexts enables Christians, in their different situations and with their different particular ways of receiving tradition, to be visibly

united in and through their witness for justice. Such unity in witness for justice, far from being triumphalist, will take the self-giving of Jesus Christ as a model for all the churches of the innermost reality and concrete life of the church today in each place.

17. The church in each regional or national situation has a particular calling from God. It must seek to respond to God's will in the light of that calling by reflection and action of a quite specific kind, depending on the specific situation. Those who brought to the Unity and Renewal consultations in Singapore, Porto Alegre and Harlem on the church's involvement in issues of justice their particular and distinctive experiences of human conflict and community gave concrete expression to this deep conviction.

18. This specificity implies at the same time that such patterns of reflection and action will not be of universal application. There should be no attempt to impose a particular pattern upon every human situation; yet all should learn from the experiences of others within their specific situations. This is not a lessening of the demand implicit in the Christian calling. For example liberation theologians in Latin America, as they develop theological insights which they believe to be important for the whole church, stress that their particular programmes are for their own Latin American situations. This does not release Christians in the North Atlantic area from a responsibility to answer the questions arising from the involvement of their governments and their international business concerns in the political and economic life of Latin American countries. The responsibility is particular; it is not the same as that of Latin American Christians; but it must be accurately discerned and in a costly way carried out.

19. In some parts of the world Christians are not in a position directly to influence governments or society as a whole because they form a tiny minority, or have to live under severe restrictions upon their social involvement. However even under these restrictions they find their own ways of making a positive witness, and are at one with the universal church in its response to God's righteousness.

20. As Christians come to a more adequate understanding of the gospel they realize how injustice breaks the fundamental relationship of communion with God and neighbour in which humankind was created, and are able to proclaim the news of God's action to set right, by atonement and by forgiveness, what has been distorted by human sin. The church lives by this action of God, proclaimed in the Bible and communicated through the Tradition of the church. It is here that the church is rooted and lives, and from here that it proceeds.

21. As Christians in different situations confront their tasks they become aware that they are not alone in their struggle. They are part of human communities in which the search for justice is urgently pursued and where often Christians need to learn from others outside the church what are the issues to be addressed. Indeed, Christians should expect in this co-operation to have their own limited vision of God's justice judged and renewed, and

their theological perspectives deepened and enriched. For example, the Singapore Consultation heard the following from the Indian context:

> The struggle for justice as practised by action groups and movements leads us also to rethink the traditional understanding of Christian mission... The mighty work of God in the world is not bound by the church and her plans. The church, instead, has to understand herself and her mission in relation to this work of God and the Spirit in the world, and has to collaborate with the Spirit in obedience to God's call and its promptings of the Spirit... [this] shows how important it is to develop today an ecclesiology based on the *mystery of the Trinity*... Similarly, an ecclesiology based on the Spirit and its working is a must today.

> *The Ecumenical Review*, Vol. 39, 3, p. 305

4. The Reality of Renewal

22. But while the church struggles to overcome human imperfections by its preaching, sacraments and pastoral nurture, it needs already to make visible the unity which manifests the victory of Christ over all that divides humankind. Such is the character of a church which is truly mystery and prophetic sign of the kingdom. The language of renewal *in* the church — renewal of the human aspects of community within the church — is a helpful way of addressing ecumenically the need, which all recognise, for improvement in the life of the church as an institution.

23. The reality of renewal in the church is rooted in the God who makes "all things new" (Rev. 21:5) and who in Jesus Christ, the Second Adam, has begun God's action of re-creation, an action which is reflected in the life of the people of God, a people in communion with God. But renewal is a process which, because of continuing human sinfulness, falls short of the radically renewed and fulfilled community of the kingdom of God. That the life of the churches is not separated from human sinfulness has been evident ever since St. Paul portrayed the congregation in Corinth. On a human plane the Christian community is subject to confusions, divisions and oppressions. These include: (i) the oppression and mistreatment of women; (ii) the wealth of the church (and its representatives) binding it to the status quo of the society in which it is set; (iii) the limiting of the freedom of knowledge and opportunity within the Christian community.

24. Nevertheless, despite human sinfulness the authority of God is mediated to God's people in such a way that, being judged, they are set free to receive the grace that initiates the process of sanctification. Christians today experience the judgment of God by recognizing those to whom Jesus gave privilege — none other than those without power or status, and this not because poverty of this nature is desirable, but because God's reign is breaking in on their behalf (Matt. 11:2-6; Luke 4:16-21). (This is why some Christians today use "justice for the poor" as their hermeneutical key for the understanding of Scripture.)

25. Ultimately there is one ground of renewal and that is Jesus Christ who, present through the Holy Spirit in word and sacrament, is the sole foundation, life-giving principle, and hope of the church. He is the origin and authority, the source of the divine power which enables the witness and mission of the church.

26. The new life in Christ must find expression in the life of the church at all levels. What does this mean in practice? While each local church or congregation will manifest the signs and marks of this renewal, it must be recognized that the congregation is set in a particular time and place, it has a context; and the marks of renewal may well be different in the many different contexts in which the church lives and offers its witness. While these local signs of renewal will be a judgment and a witness to the universal church as a communion of local churches they must not be taken as being a prescriptive model for all of them. But equally the local congregation must not succumb to the temptation of leaving renewal to the "larger church", nor leaving the struggle for justice to the communal levels of the church. The local congregation, faithful to the apostolic faith, is an expression of the church catholic. Thus it must be an expression of the new life in Christ and of his justice, thereby becoming a source of renewal of the human community.

27. This new life in Christ and his justice should also be manifested in a new life-style of Christians and their communities. Such a life-style will express today an awareness of the injustice done to creation by unlimited exploitation, and will seek to support all efforts towards a responsible stewardship of creation. Such a life-style will be a contribution to a more just sharing of the resources of this earth between rich and poor, within the framework of a new world economic order. Such a life-style will in itself become a credible witness to the readiness of the church to be used by God as an instrument for the renewal of the human community.

> ... the congregation is set in a particular time and place,
> it has a context; and the marks of renewal may
> well be different in the many different contexts in
> which the church lives and offers its witness

---

28. Particular local stories and situations offer important lessons. The consultation in Singapore, for example, heard how some congregations in India have split along the lines of the caste divisions so pervasive in that culture. As persons have been told that, because they belong to a particular caste, they are "unworthy" to bring the offering to the altar on behalf of the congregation, and as the congregation has divided into rival groups, the powers of alienation and injustice of this world have seemed victorious. Through bible study, theological reflection and prayer, Christians in this situation seek to be truly Christ's body, the church, a new humanity, rooted in God's new covenant and living in new community, where the unifying gospel of God's reconciling love in Jesus Christ may prevail (*Mid-Stream*, XXVIII, 1, pp. 1-11).

29. Another moving and powerful example comes from the experience of many African Americans in the United States. Brought as slaves to the "land of opportunity", they were subjected to the "Christianity" of their white masters as a means of control. The eucharist is intended as the central unifying act of worship; yet exclusion from the eucharist was often used to enforce a "doctrine" of racial separation and to deny full humanity to people of colour. As was said at the Harlem Consultation: "Before the rise of independent black churches, the sacraments were not experienced as a disclosure of God's transforming power, but rather as an additional means of oppression" (*Mid-Stream*, XXVIII, 4, p. 342). The scars from such abuses of Christian symbols remain to this day. Nevertheless African Americans have developed a deep and distinctive Christian faith and worship, which has enabled them to offer a powerful witness for justice, reconciliation, unity and renewal in both church and society.

30. The above examples and all other forms of discrimination and denial of human dignity and human rights are consequences of the abuse of power. As mystery, the church participates in the powerlessness of God revealed in the

life and suffering of Jesus Christ and is thus called to be in solidarity with all
who are without power. As prophetic sign the church participates in God's
action to raise up the meek and lowly and is thus called to advocate a fair
distribution of power, and the responsible exercise of power, within the life of
the human community (cf. also the reflections on power, empowerment and
service in Chapter VI, paras. 17-23).

31. In the midst of all experiences which contradict God's gift and will for
justice, the prophetic message of the church, and in particular the eucharist,
proclaims the word of God for justice and for unity:

> All kinds of injustice, racism, separation and lack of freedom are
> radically challenged when we share in the body and blood of
> Christ. Through the eucharist the all-renewing grace of God
> penetrates and restores human personality and dignity.
>
> *Baptism, Eucharist and Ministry*, Eucharist, para. 20;
> cf. in the present text Chapter I, para. 4

On the same basis the Melbourne World Mission Conference in 1980
envisioned the very structure of the eucharist as a witness for justice and unity
both within and outside the church (cf. *Your Kingdom Come*, pp. 205-206):

    i. the welcome — irrespective of race, class and gender;
    ii. the forgiveness — being freed from the past for the future;
    iii. the peace — being right with God, each other and the creation;
    iv. the sharing — the right use of resources.

Thus at the Sixth Assembly of the World Council of Churches it was affirmed
that "the aspect of Christian unity which has been most striking to us here in
Vancouver is that of a eucharistic vision. Christ — the life of the world —
unites heaven and earth, God and world, spiritual and secular" (*Gathered for
Life*, p. 44). Such a vision renders even more scandalous the fact that
Christians are not able to come together at the Lord's table, and highlights the
aim of the WCC "to call the churches to the goal of visible unity in one faith
and one eucharistic fellowship" (WCC Constitution, III, "Functions and
Purposes", 1; cf. the discussion of the goal of this study in Chapter I, para 9).

The connection between unity and justice makes it
necessary to ask of every expression of visible
unity: "Does it promote justice in the light of the
gospel of Jesus Christ, both within the church and
the world?" And secondly, "Does it foster the
engagement of the church in God's work for justice?"

---

32. The experience of renewal and the search for unity must not remain at the personal and collegial levels, but at a communal level judge and inspire all discussions of plans for making unity visible. The criterion by which the vision of the unity which Christians seek will be judged is nothing less than the radical renewal and fulfilment of the human community. The connection between unity and justice makes it necessary to ask of every expression of visible unity: "Does it promote justice in the light of the gospel of Jesus Christ, both within the church and the world?" And secondly, "Does it foster the engagement of the church in God's work for justice?" Positively speaking the witness must be heard of many Christians who from various denominations, joined together in specific circumstances to witness against injustice, have received a foretaste of that unity which is the gift of God. This confirms the witness of Scripture: "Seek *first* God's kingdom... and all these things shall be yours as well" (Matt. 6:33).

5. The True Glory

33. Jesus' own total obedience took him along the way of the cross; his true glory was manifested in his death and in his rising (John 17 and 20). He bids his disciples to "take up the cross" and follow him on a way which involves suffering, yet a suffering in hope, even now shared and made sustainable by the prayers of the whole church. Both for those who suffer exclusion, powerlessness, and injustice and for those who suffer in the struggle to bring justice to the oppressed, there is a sure and certain hope that in the end God will overcome and God's kingdom will be established, a kingdom of which Christians are a part. Then, and then only, will the unity of the church and the renewal of human community be visible in their fullness and their concreteness.

Questions for Reflection and Discussion

1. How do Christians in your society engage in questions of justice? Do they react to specific issues in different ways, or do they agree?

2. What influences them most in shaping their reaction (for example the Bible, church teaching, tradition, cultural attitudes, etc.)?

CHAPTER V

Unity and Renewal and the
Community of Women and Men

1. In the setting of God's kingdom Christian community is brought to fulfillment. God's salvation is realized as love which essentially expresses itself in new community. This process is seen in Acts (2:42-47; 4:32-35) where following baptism and the gift of the Holy Spirit the believers devote themselves to living together in Christian community.

2. Again and again in the history of the church, Christians have needed to be called anew to live out in community the implications of the gospel. Many of the New Testament epistles address situations in which those who have personally responded to the preaching of the gospel are facing problems in relating to one another in the life of the church. This gives to these letters their regular structure of teaching about God's saving work in Christ followed by a description of the implications of salvation for human relationships. So, for example, in the Letter to the Galatians, Paul teaches the purpose of the law and the coming of faith in Christ (2:15-3:26), and then describes how Jesus gives to Jews and Gentiles, slaves and free, men and women, a common access to salvation. A new relationship to Christ and to one another is established for all of them (3:27-29). On that basis a common life of freedom in the Spirit comes to fruition and new community is created. As mature Christians they will then bear one another's burdens (6:1-10); and Paul ends by adding in his own handwriting the insistence that what matters is being a *new creation* (6:15). This new creation is experienced and realised in the new community "in Christ".

3. Paul and the other apostles, and all who have followed them, in calling women and men to live in Christian community have emphasized that there is a continual process of growth to maturity under the guidance and grace of the Holy Spirit. Knowing that the Lord is here and that his Spirit is with us, Christians have confidence in God, as children trust a loving parent; that confidence gives confidence also for their relationship with others, the strength for all circumstances which derives from the Lord who empowers them (Phil. 4:13).

4. A Christian community lives in anticipation of the kingdom of God. In every communion service it recalls the basis of its life in the death of Christ and his living presence until his coming again. Such a community is aware of the weakness and brokenness in its human relationships. Thus what is said in this chapter about the community of women and men needs to be read in connection with what is said in Chapter IV about justice; the community of women and men in both church and society is still marred by evident injustices from which the church struggles to emerge. Yet the church as bearer of the mystery of salvation knows that its relationships are now grounded in Christ, who can and does transform them. This chapter explores the implications of this basic understanding of Christian community for the community of women and men.

1. The Calling of Women and Men to Christian Community

5. A true community of women and men is God's gift and promise for humanity, which is created "in God's image" — male and female (Gen. 1:27); and the church, as prophetic sign of that which God desires for women and men, is called to embody that community in its own life. Today Christians from many traditions look together for a more complete and authentic community of women and men.

6. The domination of women by men does not belong to human community as intended in God's creation (Gen. 2:23) but to the consequences of sin, which distort the community of women and men as well as the relationship between human beings and nature (Gen. 3:16-19).

> The domination of women by men does not belong to
> human community as intended in God's creation...
> but to the consequences of sin...

---

7. The division between male and female raises profound questions of theology and anthropology: questions of what it means that we are not simply human, but human *as male or female*. There are fundamental questions concerning, for example, the relation between being and function, between biology and identity: How far do the distinctive biological functions of women and men determine their roles in society and in the church? How far is gender constitutive of identity? How far should difference of gender determine differences in status and role?

8. Although very different answers are given to such questions, Christians are agreed that in a right relationship between women and men reconciliation is experienced and the full humanity of both women and men is expressed. They believe that God has called Christ's body, the church, to be a place of such reconciliation. As mystery the church participates in God's desire for

fullness of life for all humanity, and is thus called to enable and nurture the full exercise of the gifts of all God's people, women and men. As prophetic sign the church participates in God's reconciling will for humanity and is thus called to show forth, in its own life, how one of the most profound and pervasive divisions within creation — that between male and female — may be overcome in the common belonging of men and women "in Christ".

9. Christians approach questions concerning men and women in Christian community from their fundamental conviction that God out of love for God's creation has given the Son, so that all might have life in abundance (John 10:10). In Christ all are led into a new community, one which is already a foretaste of the kingdom of God (see Chapter II, para. 34).

10. One may ask why the community which God has promised has still — after 2000 years — to be seen and experienced fully. This is in part because of continuing human sin, in part because of changes and developments in the human situation itself. As members of the body of Christ, Christians look to Scripture and Tradition to focus the light and life which the incarnation brings, and this is a continuing search. In each community each generation, inspired by the Holy Spirit, comes "in Christ" to the Father, seeking through reflection and prayer the resolution of the issues with which it is faced.

11. While Christians seek to understand the changing world using all available resources (including, for example, historical study, psychological observation of the human condition, and sociological analysis), they look ultimately for the theological and spiritual implications and opportunities in the challenges which confront humanity.

12. The search for a more complete and authentically Christian community of women and men is a demanding one: it requires ecclesiological study from the authentic perspective of many different confessions; theological reflection on the experience of women and men in many different cultural and confessional contexts; the trust which opens one to the insights of other Christians, however different and challenging these may be; the courage to repent of ideas and practices which distort and deny a true community of women and men; and the readiness to respond to new understandings of the human situation with innovative ideas and attitudes.

13. Ecumenical sharing, discussion and reflection (through, for example, the study programme on The Community of Women and Men in the Church, culminating in the Sheffield Consultation in 1981, and the Unity and Renewal consultations on issues of the Community of Women and Men in Prague, 1985, and Benin, 1988) have brought together the experiences of women and men from many cultures and Christian traditions. These experiences are often of broken community and of oppressive human relationships which deny that fullness of life which God wills for all people. It is in recognition of these negative experiences that the churches are seeking for positive advance through common efforts, including the Ecumenical Decade of the Churches in Solidarity with Women (1988-1998), and this study on Unity and Renewal.

14. Work on issues of Christian community, and their final resolution, will necessarily take place in the context of the local church, through the insights which have been and are being given by the Holy Spirit and its redeeming and recreative power. Resolution must also occur at a more universal level, as Christians seek, through the power and witness of a more complete and authentic community of women and men, the unity of the church and the renewal of human community.

15. Experiences of community occur in different contexts and are influenced by different cultural and economic factors. Here it is possible only to indicate some common threads in the human condition which challenge Christians seeking a renewed community of women and men today.

2. Some Challenges of a Changing Situation

A. CHANGES IN SOCIETY

16. There have been and continue to be significant changes in the situation of contemporary women, although the speed and extent of change varies greatly. Wherever change occurs in the situations of women, the lives of men are also affected.

17. In many places women and men still struggle for basic human rights. In much of the world women now have legal equality with men (although this is still lacking in a number of countries). And even when "equality" has been achieved legally, it may not be realized in the actual situations and daily lives of many women.

18. Developments in the field of health have crucial effects for women, although here again there are significant differences, particularly between developed and developing countries. Increasingly, however, reduced infant mortality rates result in less pressure on women to bear many children in order to ensure the continuation of particular families and of the whole human race. At the same time, more effective means of birth control enable women, particularly in the West, to make more choices in the field of human reproduction. Coupled with generally increased life expectancy this means that, for significant numbers of women, there are now greater opportunities to work outside the home, whether in traditional areas such as agriculture or in paid employment.

19. Where educational opportunities for women have increased, women have gained enhanced knowledge and skills, and new aspirations, which encourage them to participate in the world outside the home, including the world of employment. At the same time economic pressures on the family, as well as, in many countries, increasing urbanization and industrialization, also encourage — if not force — women to seek employment.

20. Women's experience in the workplace is often negative. They generally receive lower wages than men and have fewer opportunities to exercise responsibility and leadership. They often experience their "freedom" for paid employment as an added burden, because they are expected not only to work for necessary income but to continue to raise their children and to look after the home as well.

Both men and women are vulnerable to stereotypes
and patterns which hinder communication and
co-operation in church and society

---

21. Changing conditions and chances often make the search for a true community of women and men more difficult. For example, an unfavourable economic climate means less job security, and this may generate conflicts

because men and women are forced to compete for scarce jobs and wages. Yet while in some situations women and men are forced into competition and seem to struggle against each other for justice and liberation, in other situations women and men work *together* in solidarity on behalf of the oppressed, seeking freedom and justice for others as for themselves.

22. When the variety of roles open to women is explored, it becomes apparent that the struggle of women for justice is interwoven with other struggles, and that women can find themselves in conflict with other women in the areas of racism, class or national rivalries.

B. CHANGES IN MARRIAGE AND THE FAMILY

23. In many countries and societies there is a lack of mutuality in the intimate relationship of marriage, due in part to fixed and inherited expectations and roles associated with being a husband or a wife. This lack of mutuality is often exaggerated by local laws and customs associated with property, inheritance, and sexuality. Within the institutions of marriage and family life women from many situations suffer a lack of freedom, or of partnership in decision-making. On the other hand, women who are single and those who do not have children often experience discrimination and marginalization.

24. In many countries and cultures traditional patterns of marriage and family life have undergone and are still undergoing change. In some cases the concept of marriage is even challenged and redefined. Although changes in traditional patterns and institutions are welcomed by many, others feel a sense of loss as familiar roles and expectations no longer prevail. Not all women want to change their traditional role in the family, which they see as having an essential value and dignity.

25. Especially in Western countries, there is an increased possibility for both women and men to remain unmarried, although for many marriage is still the norm and expectation. Divorce rates have increased in many places, as have the number of single parent families, and this has serious consequences for the lives of children. Economic and social factors may weaken marriage and family institutions; for example, men may have to live apart from the family in order to find employment, or parents may be unable to afford adequate care to their children, or even be forced to abandon them.

26. Men are becoming increasingly aware of the destructive pressures which they face. Especially in Europe and North America men find the present situation distressing. They experience more frequently the breaking up of marriage and the loss of children, and must deal with changes in attitudes towards women, as well as their altered role and place in the family, church and the economic arena; all this brings insecurity and fear to many men.

C. THE HOPE OF LIBERATION FOR WOMEN AND MEN

27. Both men and women are vulnerable to stereotypes and patterns which hinder communication and co-operation in church and society. The home,

the workplace, and the church are all affected by the perceptions that label women as weak, emotional, vulnerable, submissive, and unable to "hold their own" in the competitive workplace, while attributing to men the qualities of physical prowess, self-control, leadership ability, and rationality.

28. Freedom to speak, contribute, and participate in decision-making are today widely understood as being essential elements of true membership and partnership in community. The realization of renewed community is hampered by imperfect structures. Exclusiveness, oppressive power and authority, lack of political rights, demeaning or patronizing language and the attitudes it presupposes, paternalism, predetermined roles, and lack of mutuality all reinforce unyielding structures and patterns that exclude women from full personhood, from leadership and from real participation in the decision-making processes of the life of a community.

29. In many respects the contemporary women's movement has helped to break down destructive and limiting stereotypes, and to create the freedom for women and men to exhibit the attributes, qualities and skills that benefit human community in all areas of life. These are advances in *human* liberation.

3. Christian Perspectives

A. THE NEWNESS OF THE GOSPEL

30. Christian faith is deeply rooted in the joyful message of the gospel that Jesus Christ by his suffering and death has freed us from the powers of sin and all its destructive consequences for human life. Through the power of the Holy Spirit the gift of this freedom opens women and men to the love of God, poured into their hearts and granting them life in a wholly new dimension of relationship with God and with one another.

31. The same love of God which is the life of the Holy Trinity itself, and has been poured out since the beginning of the world, becomes now the distinctive quality which marks the community of believers, making them sisters and brothers, equal partners who share, in solidarity with one another, all their gifts and needs.

32. Christians are all one in Christ (John 17:21-26); there is among them no longer slave nor free (Gal. 3:28). It is Jesus Christ himself who has shown them the pattern of his own lordship, through a servant's gesture — by washing the feet of the disciples (John 13:1-17) — thereby establishing the new order of love, both in contrast to and in fulfillment of the law of the old covenant.

33. This is also shown in many other biblical texts in which Jesus demonstrates for all women and men a way of relationship which is honest, respectful, and open to growth and change, a way pointing to a life in new community within the kingdom of God. For example, Jesus' conversation with the Samaritan woman (John 4:7-26) shows him encountering her in ways which, on many counts, go far beyond the predominant male perspective of his time and place.

He offers neither judgment nor flattery, he listens and responds frankly and personally, and the woman is enabled to see herself and Jesus afresh and to take new steps in faith. The desperate plea and bold retort of the Syro-Phoenician woman (Mark 7:24-30) are heard and answered by Jesus.

B. RELATIONSHIPS "IN CHRIST"

34. In Christian tradition men and women are created in the image of God, who has been revealed as a communion of love of the Father, of the Son and of the Holy Spirit. Men and women as images of the triune God are, therefore, instrinsically relational. They become fully human as they live a life that reflects the relations that exist among the three persons of the Trinity. This can be done only in Christ and through the power of the Holy Spirit.

35. The creation narratives of Genesis picture humanity created "in God's image" (in the *imago dei*) as male and female. Each person, man or woman, is a sign to the other of the Lord of creation, a sign that all are to live their lives in conformity to the nature and will of God. It is clear, despite the teaching of some theologians in the past and the all-too-frequent practice of the church as human institution, that there is no "secondary" *imago dei* for women, and thus no superior nature or favoured role for men.

36. In Genesis 1 and 2 the relationship between men and women is described in terms of mutuality and communion. In church and society today men and women relate to each other in many different ways — as members of different generations in a family, or as brothers and sisters, as friends, as co-workers — as well as in marriage. Mutuality and communion should mark all these varied relationships.

37. The family, in some Christian traditions, is called to be a "little church". Parallel to this, the Report from the Benin consultation speaks of the "sacramental character" of marriage (p. 6). In the family one hopes to find a stable environment in which the procreation and nurture of children can take place, so that they may increase in their knowledge of the love of God and in reverence for God's commandments. In marriage husband and wife may grow together in such a way that each enables, indeed encourages, the other to grow in knowledge and understanding of, and so in communion with, God. The reality for both marriage and the family is often tragically different, marked by brokenness in relationships and hopes not realized. What light and life comes from reflection on present experience with the help of Scripture and Tradition?

38. From a theological perspective, the relationships among God, men and women, and the creation have been broken and this has resulted in patterns of dominance and submission between husband and wife, and between human beings and creation. The coming of Christ then breaks the cycle of sin which has distorted or destroyed the gift of human relationships, including the institution of marriage. In Christ the pattern of dominance and submission is shattered; women have been released from the aspects of "law" which had long oppressed them. Their theological status is now that of the "new creature" — no longer inferior and submissive. Men too are freed, in their case from the need to dominate, and can develop their own gifts fully within the community of the new creation. This re-creation should be realized in all human relationships.

39. Christians today are seeking how to understand anew the witness of Scripture and Tradition on human relationships, and particularly on marriage. Texts such as Ephesians 5:21-6:9, Colossians 3:18-4:1, and 1 Peter 3:1-7 raise questions as to how such teachings apply to present situations.

40. In Ephesians 5:21-6:9 human relationships are to be understood afresh in the light of Christ's love and self-giving for the church; this love is the primary reality, which illumines the relationships, rather than the relationships being used as analogies for the divine love. Thus the writer refers the

> The... group has provided a place for both women and men to explore, in a creative and secure environment, what it means to be made in the image of God. Especially for some of the women, involvement has led them to a new liberation through the Gospel, with a new vision of God as ultimately beyond the finite language of maleness or fatherhood. This has led many to a new discovery of their own fundamental worth as created in the image of God, acceptable in God's sight and as equal and valued partners in a renewed community with their brothers in the faith.
>
> Flora Winfield on the Oxford Women's Liturgy Group

passage in Genesis 2:24 (about leaving one's parents in order to be joined to one's wife) to Christ and the church. Once this basis of the argument is grasped it becomes clear that the relationships of husband and wife, parent and child, master and slave, all commonly seen in terms of power of the first over the second, are to be transformed by the self-giving love of Christ. It is in the new manner in which Christ is head, in the new manner in which the church is subject to Christ, and not according to the customary human patterns, that relationships are to develop within the Christian community. All power and relationships are to be transformed on the basis of Christ's love for the church and the church's love for its Lord. Such transformation was not necessarily completed at the close of the New Testament period. For instance, the transformed relationship of Christian master and Christian slave within the institution of slavery, described in Paul's letter to Philemon, eventually — after many centuries — was one factor that led churches to repudiate slavery entirely, and to work for its abolition.

C. MINISTRIES OF THE CHURCH

41. Another complex set of issues concerns the ministries of women and the question of the ordination of women. The range and diversity of questions raised, and positions taken, can readily be seen by comparing the Reports and other texts from the several parts of the WCC "Community of Women and Men in the Church" Study (1977-1981), the Roman Catholic declaration *Inter Insigniores* on the ordination of women (1977), and the Report of the Pan-Orthodox Conference on Rhodes in 1988 on "The Place of the Woman in the Orthodox Church and the Question of the Ordination of Women".

42. The Unity and Renewal consultations at Prague and Benin, and the Steering Group meeting in Leuenberg, have necessarily addressed these issues and have recognized agreement (a) on the necessity to see the ordained ministry and *episcope* in the church as gifts of God, to serve pastoral upbuilding of the Christian community; and (b) on the many ministries of women and men which are recognized in all the churches as charisms exercised in the

life of the church. They have equally recognized (c) the need for biblical and historical study on the issues and (d) the fact that there is no consensus among the churches on the question of ordaining women to a full ministry of word and sacrament/priesthood. Paragraphs 43-46 below briefly express our agreement on (a) and (b) above. Paragraphs 47-51 indicate the *questions* (*not* answers) of the hermeneutical debate raised by (c). Paragraphs 52-53 refer to the pressure and anxieties produced by dividedness about (d).

43. The people of God (the *laos tou theou*) includes *all* members of the church — clergy and lay — and therefore hierarchy cannot be seen in opposition to laity, nor as precluding the equality of all persons before God. False notions of power (see VI, 17-23) have prevented the exercise of the full diversity of gifts in the one body of Christ by limiting the level of participation allowed to women — and to many men — in much of the institutional life of the churches.

44. Much work must be done to reconcile apparent "opposites" found in different streams of biblical language and embodied today in different understandings of church polity. This is needed to recover both the fullness of the royal priesthood of all believers and an understanding of "hierarchy" as the exercise of an authority grounded in that of Jesus, the servant Lord, and in the love of the Triune God.

45. Today all lay people should be encouraged and enabled to recognize their gifts within the full diversity of lay ministries. Greater participation of all lay people in a greater range of ministries would itself lead to major changes within the churches' life. The ministry of the laity is not restricted to the internal life of the church, but is expressed especially as Christians live and work in society.

46. Within the diversity of the ministry of the *laity* the work of Christian women — whether as mothers, homemakers, church workers in society, or in secular professions and employment — needs to be affirmed.

47. The place of women within the *ordained* ministries of the church is a complex issue. Historically speaking, the reduction of the multiplicity and diversity of orders for men and women in church life (for example widows, virgins, deaconesses, readers, sub-deacons, and so on) has led to an over-emphasis on roles exercised by men, and in some churches to the almost exclusive limitation to men of roles involving governance and decision-making. Thus while the place of male deacons in worship and leadership functions has become increasingly prominent, some forms of *diakonia* ("service" in its humbler aspects!) have been relegated primarily to women (cf. Chapter VI, para. 21). Today there are moves to reinstitute a broader range of orders within the life of the church.

48. Biblically speaking, in light of the more comprehensive context reflected in paragraph 43 above for considering ministry in the church, it is now possible to look with new insight to the New Testament references to the roles of women. For example, the positive image of a Lydia (Acts 16:14-15), a Phoebe (Rom. 16:1-2) or a Chloe (1 Cor. 1:11) may be set alongside passages which seem more negative.

49. But the proper interpretation of the biblical texts related to the ministries of women in the life of the church remains a complex issue. A fresh look at some passages concerning worship (in particular, 1 Cor. 11:3-16) shows that they do not *a priori* exclude women's activity in worship; indeed they seek to ensure that women have adequate "space" for praying and prophesying. Yet in recognizing this many Christians emphasize that God the creator has delighted in honouring men and women with special, different gifts and responsiblities, and conclude that they must be sensitive to the need to maintain a certain distinction between them.

Some churches ordain both men and women, others ordain only men. Differences on this issue raise obstacles to the mutual recognition of ministries. But those obstacles must not be regarded as substantive hindrance for further efforts towards mutual recognition. Openness to each other holds the possibility that the Spirit may well speak to one church through the insights of another. Ecumenical consideration, therefore, should encourage, not restrain, the facing of this question.

Baptism, Eucharist and Ministry

---

50. Other passages refer to women in relation to the question of preaching or teaching within the church. Paul in 2 Corinthians 11:3-4 refers to Eve being deceived by the serpent, and hopes that his readers will not similarly be "led astray"; but here the image of Eve includes all whom he addresses, both women *and* men, just as elsewhere the image of Adam includes both men and women. By contrast 1 Timothy 2:11-15 emphasises the priority of Adam over Eve, who "was deceived and became a transgressor". There is a clear injunction in 1 Timothy 2:12 which, taken literally, would preclude many ministries performed by women within the churches today and in the past, including the ministries of many women acknowledged by the church as saints.

51. For many scholars and theologians as they now study the New Testament and Tradition these texts raise several fundamental questions of interpretation. These include the following:

— Are the Pauline passages so conditioned by their specific cultural context (the Jewish-Hellenistic culture of the first century C.E.) that they no longer apply in the different culture(s) of later times?

— If the passages do apply universally, do they reflect an order of creation instituted by God which continues to preclude the ordination of women to priestly ministry? Or are they a time-conditioned response to distortions of the order of creation caused by human sinfulness, and therefore no longer applicable in the light of what we have come to recognize as the fundamental equality of women and men in Christ?

- If the latter is the case, has the new order of redemption inaugurated by Jesus Christ overcome these consequences of human sinfulness so as to open all ministries in the church to both men and women?

- In addressing these hermeneutical issues how should one relate Tradition, and its expression of the equality of women and men in terms of their equal access to salvation in Christ, to distinctions of appropriate function in the ministries of the church?

- How are the various particularities of Jesus' humanity — his being born a Jew, at a particular time, speaking (a) particular language(s), being male — related to the representation of the risen Christ in the life of the church? What is the significance for Christians today of the traditional emphasis on the last of these factors, namely that Jesus was male?

52. It is very difficult even to formulate these questions in a way which does not prejudge the answers from one point of view or another. The question of the ordination of women remains divisive within the ecumenical movement. Dialogue on the issue is essential for continued good relations between churches who are experiencing this divisiveness; an issue such as this cannot be set aside, since it clearly affects, in different ways according to different church practises, the relationships of women and men in the church.

53. As the relations between churches form part of the search for the fullness of Christian unity in truth, each church, whether it now ordains women or not, needs to study seriously, praying for the guidance of the Holy Spirit, the ministries of the church in the light of Scripture and Tradition. To engage in such a study does not presuppose one particular result; it requires only a willingness to discern the truth and to find the right way and time of responding to it, wherever it leads. Such discernment, in this case, will involve consideration of the place of the issue of the ordination of women in relation to other problems and opportunities, and an estimation of its significance for the life of the church as a sign for the renewal of human community.

The fact that the issues of the community of women
and men affect every human society... makes
them a special testing place for the Christian claim
to have received a truth in Christ which
illuminates all human experience

---

4. The Community of Women and Men: Challenge and Hope

54. In the church the wounds of disappointed hope and defeated endeavour, the brokenness caused by racism, sexism, ageism and all other barriers between human beings are healed when, in Christ, Christian women and

men, from their own experience of brokenness and healing, of division and re-creation, reach out to others in need.

55. The fact that the issues of the community of women and men affect every human society, across all the diversities of nation, race and political structure, makes them a special testing place for the Christian claim to have received a truth in Christ which illuminates all human experience. The church as mystery and prophetic sign is called to show in a particular way how women and men are in God's image and likeness.

56. The God who created us as women and men calls us into community. The Christ who identifies with our suffering calls us to become his body. The Spirit who empowers us to witness and serve sends us forth as God's agents, co-workers in a new heaven and a new earth.

Questions for Reflection and Discussion

1. Are any significant changes concerning the roles and relationship of women and men happening in your society?

2. How do you experience issues of the community of women and men in your church?

CHAPTER VI

Discipleship and Community

1. The source and centre of Christian community is its life in the risen Christ. It is a community of renewal, a pilgrim people, women, men and children called out in faith, journeying by the light of a star, warmed by a pillar of fire and fed enough bread for each day of the journey.

2. Scripture and Christian history offer rich resources for those who seek to live in Christian community today. For example Mary, the mother of the Lord, is an important example for all who seek to understand the full dimensions of life in Christian community.

— Mary receives the Word of God and responds directly from her faith, believing in the fulfillment of God's promise despite its seeming strangeness (Luke 1:26-38).

— Mary shares with Elizabeth the good news of the wonderful works of God on behalf of his people and praises God for all he has done for her and for all the poor and lowly (Luke 1:46-55).

— Mary meditates on the meaning of Jesus' birth, and suffers danger and exile for his sake, and strives to understand him as he grows to maturity (Luke 2:19; Matt. 2:13-23; Luke 2:41-51).

— Mary struggles, with the rest of Jesus' immediate family, to understand the full implications of his way of self-giving service and to learn the basis of a true relationship with the Christ (Mark 3:31-35; Luke 18:19-20, cf. Matt. 12:46-50, Luke 8:19-21).

— Mary is lost to sight among the men and women following her son until she re-emerges to stand under the cross and to follow the body to the tomb (John 19:25-27; Matt. 27:55-61).

— Finally Mary is among the disciples, women and men, in the upper room before Pentecost who "with one accord devoted themselves to prayer" and waited for the "promise of the Father". With them she is filled with the Holy Spirit and so is called into new community (Acts 1:12-14, 2:1-4, 2:42, 4:32-35).

> ## I often think of Mary
>
> I suffered so much when they arrested my son. When I went to ask where he was, they said they didn't know. I searched and searched, but couldn't find him. Finally his corpse appeared, his head in one place and his body in another. I fainted when I saw him. I thought of how Jesus' mother also suffered when they told her that her son had been arrested. Surely she went searching for him and later saw him die and then helped to bury him. That is why, I think, she understands my sorrow and helps me to go on.
>
> An El Salvadoran woman, speaking on Mother's Day, 1983

3. As at Pentecost, Christians today need the help of the Holy Spirit to hear together what God is saying to all God's people. Issues concerning the promotion of justice and the community of women and men necessarily involve reflection on language and on issues of power, empowerment and service.

1. Language and Community

4. Language is a primary means through which individuals and communities — including Christians and christian communities — communicate with one another and shape, share and defend their identity and deepest values. But particular languages may have forms and be used in ways which either include persons or groups within, or exclude them from, community. Thus the sensitive use of language can be a powerful tool for upbuilding the community; but an insensitive use of language may reflect stereotypes and reinforce sexism, racism, ageism, and other sources of alienation and injustice, thus harming the community.

5. Languages both shape and are shaped by the communities in which they are used. A language reinforces the beliefs and attitudes of a community, while at the same time changing and developing in response to changes and developments in the community. Furthermore, human languages vary greatly among themselves, for instance in the ways in which they express gender. They may be more or less inclusive: some have a greater variety of forms for distinguishing feminine and masculine terms, as well as pronouns referring to both genders, while in some little distinction is made gramatically between genders.

6. Careful attention must be paid to the distinctive possibilities and problems of expression in the specific language(s) being used. This is especially important in a multi-lingual context. Issues and problems particular to one dominant language, for example English, should not be projected into other

linguistic contexts. But neither should their absence in other languages prevent problems being recognized, and addressed, within communities for which English is the prevailing tongue. Especially in international and ecumenical contexts greater care should be taken not to let the use of language become an instrument of domination.

7. In many cases the search for justice and for a fuller community of women and men has led to a quest for more inclusive language, and to a readiness to change some inherited forms of language. Because languages themselves are not static, but change and develop over time, certain words and phrases which previously were experienced as embracing all persons within a church or Christian community may no longer be experienced as expressing the full catholicity of the people of God. When a significant portion of a Christian community no longer feels itself addressed by specific terms and phrases — or indeed feels excluded by them — then the urgent attention of the whole community is needed. The language of a Christian community, above all, should upbuild the life of the community and its members in their full diversity.

8. At the same time it must be recognized that where language is already inclusive this has not necessarily resulted in inclusive community. Language and its relationship to diverse elements within community remain a complex issue, both in respect to particular social and cultural groupings and to the community of women and men.

9. As Christians search for a fuller community a growing complex of issues has arisen around the use of language in the life of the church, in theology and worship. The language used in speaking of and addressing God, the language used in translating the Scriptures, the language of theology and worship, the language used in hymns, have all come under scrutiny.

When a significant portion of a Christian community
no longer feels itself addressed by specific terms
and phrases — or indeed feels excluded by them
— then the urgent attention of the
whole community is needed

---

10. These issues of language involve fundamental theological questions and cannot be resolved apart from them. For example, theologians agree that God cannot be contained within human thought-forms and language, and that the use of masculine terminology such as "Father" and "Lord" does not mean that God is "male". An African participant at the Benin consultation noted that ways of thinking and speaking about God which seek to encompass more aspects of the divine nature can foster a more complete and authentic community of women and men: "It is because Africans in our traditional

thought forms take seriously the feminine attributes of God that we should see women as not inferior to men, but see women and men as created to complement each other".

11. Yet complex and difficult problems may arise in "translating" this awareness into practice, particularly in languages, such as English, which use masculine grammatical forms ("he", "him") only and specifically to refer to male living things. Careful and sensitive work must be done in relating current linguistic perspectives and possibilities to the legitimate values of traditional forms of language.

> A mother feeds her child with her milk,
> but our beloved mother Jesus
> feeds us with himself.
>
> Julian of Norwich,
> *Revelations of Divine Love*

12. Some traditional terms used of God (such as "Father" and "Lord") have today become problematic for some Christians, who feel that they inevitably imply, within the linguistic context of contemporary English, the "maleness" of God. Because of its importance in the theology and history of the church the traditional trinitarian formula is of special significance in this discussion. Here some seek language which is, they believe, more expressive within the context of contemporary English of the full reality of the transcendent God who is beyond all language. For example, one approach has been to supplement the "masculine" language of "Father" and "Son" with terms such as "Creator" and "Redeemer", which do not imply gender. However, this implies a different understanding of the relationship between the three persons of the Godhead, and this too causes difficulties.

13. The Bible itself uses a great variety of images for God, including a significant number of feminine images. For example, God is imaged as king (Ps. 99:1,4, 47:2), shepherd (Ps. 23:1, 80:1), father (Ps. 68:5), as a warrior (Ps. 35:1-3), a rock (Ps. 62:6, 95:1), a stronghold (Ps. 61:3), a fortress (Ps. 71:3); and also as a mother (Isa. 46:3-4, 49:14-15; Hos. 11:4), a female eagle (Ex. 19:4; Deut. 32:11; Ps. 36:7), a mother hen (Matt. 23:37), a midwife (Ps. 22:9-10; Isa. 66:9), as one who both creates and gives birth (Deut. 32:18). In Luke the image of the shepherd searching for a lost sheep (Luke 15:3-7) is paralleled by the image of the housewife searching for a lost coin (Luke 15:8-10). Contemporary theological and liturgical language has often ignored this diversity of imagery, which many feel could be helpful in suggesting the full reality and transcendence of God and in avoiding possible distortions and limitations in speaking of God.

14. Problems may arise in translating the Scriptures from one language into another. Modern languages may offer possibilities of expression not foreseen by the biblical writers, while on the other hand the original biblical languages often contain a richness of meaning that is not adequately conveyed in translations. For example, in the Old Testament God is frequently described by the phrase "merciful and compassionate" (Deut. 4:31; Neh. 9:17; Ps. 78:38, 111:4, 145:8; Joel 2:13; Jonah 4:2). The adjective translated as "merciful" is in Hebrew *rahum* and derives from the noun *rehem*, meaning "womb" or "uterus", thus giving in the Hebrew connotations which are not easily expressed in translation into other languages.

15. In the areas of worship and hymnody the problems raised by the effort to use inclusive language involve also considerations of poetry, rhythm and metre. Here it is particularly important to be sensitive to the distinctive qualities and possibilities of the particular language being used.

16. Christians in each place must continue to reflect on the issues of language and its use, being sensitive to the need for language which is both faithful to Scripture and Tradition, and compelling and convincing to men and women today. They must ensure that their own words shape, sustain and communicate that Christian community grounded in *God's* Word for all men and women, Jesus Christ.

2. Power, Empowerment and Service

17. Life in community — including Christian community — inevitably involves the exercise of power. The proper understanding and use of power is creative within the life of the community, but power is often used in a way that distorts life within the community and prevents the full development of the gifts of all its members. The misuse of power by self-seeking individuals is a destructive expression of human sinfulness, one which negates many sincere efforts towards true Christian and human community. Thus striving for a correct understanding of power and its exercise is fundamental to the search for both justice and new forms of the community of women and men.

18. The basic choice is between seeing power as quantitative and seeing it as qualitative. If power is quantitative, then a gain in power for one person must mean a loss of power for someone else; if power is qualitative it can be shared, in such a way that more power becomes available for the growth of individuals and their community. Hierarchy — in any church — must be a conscientious, intentional exercise, in love, of such *qualitative* power according to the model offered by Jesus.

19. Thus the words and example of Jesus continue to challenge and correct his followers in their tendency to distort relationships by the way in which they understand power and its exercise. The understanding of power influences the understanding of church structures, and the conduct of ministries and relationships in the church. Where service and ministry are themselves affected by a limiting, merely quantitative concept of power, both the church's own inner life and its mission to the world are inevitably flawed. This is true both of hierarchically-ordered churches and those which have a different form of decision-making, for in all churches there is necessarily some exercise of power and thus the possibility of its distortion.

20. One negative result of the distorted exercise of power is often the fixing of clearly marked-out and unchangeable roles for those who lead and those who are led. The relationship remains static and closed to new ways of thinking and behaving, and emphasizes the difference between the parties involved: there is giver and receiver, minister and ministered to. Mutuality and exchange are therefore blocked, to the injuring of both personal wholeness and the life and mission of the whole community — the gifts of whose members may be unused, unacknowledged, or undiscovered.

21. False notions of power and its exercise also distort the crucial Christian concept of service. All Christian communities hold that Jesus taught his

disciples a way of humble service, even to the washing of one another's feet or the taking of the last place. However, in practise "service" often means different things for different groups within the community: for example, for women it often means activities such as serving tables, while for men it means positions of leadership (cf. Chapter V, para. 47). Here the gospel invitation to all persons to serve has broken down into static relationships of power on one side and powerlessness on the other. This situation has been encouraged by a false "piety" of submission for women and other non-decision-makers, enjoined through overt preaching, biblical exegesis and spiritual direction, and through what is simply "expected" in the life of the church. This is experienced as being parallel to unjust secular patterns of relationship.

22. In seeking to correct such distortions the Christian community takes its cue from Jesus himself. In the Gospel record all contacts with Jesus are portrayed as opening the way to more abundant life for both individuals and communities. He is a master who does not "lord it" over others, a servant without servility. When James and John request a special status in the coming kingdom Jesus does not berate their wrongheadedness, but shows them that they are thinking like the pagan political rulers who do "lord it" over their subjects. He sets before them an alternate model of power in the mission of the Son of man to serve rather than to be served, and to give his life as a ransom for many (Mark 10:35-45).

23. The church is called to follow, through the help of the Holy Spirit, this model in shaping its own life as a Christian community. In so doing it will become a sign and instrument for the renewal of the human community, a compelling witness to God's wish for abundant life for all women and men.

Happiness is not to be found in dominating one's fellows, or in wanting to have more than his weaker brethren, or in possessing riches and riding roughshod over his inferiors. No one can become an imitator of God like that, for such things are wholly alien to God's greatness.

The Epistle to Diognetus

---

3. The Life of Christian Communion

24. Christian community has assumed very diverse forms throughout history in the different cultural situations where the gospel has been planted. The marks of Christian community may vary from one historical, cultural and geographical setting to another. What is fundamental is a pattern of the community seeking the source and goal of its life in Christ, and of persistent caring, in the spirit of Christ, for others both in the community and in the world. Such a renewed community rejoices over people's gifts and enables them to offer them in service to the church and to society. These gifts are not only those of listening and caring, of challenging and putting right, of justice,

peace and joy, but also new gifts, offered through the experience of transformation through the Spirit.

25. In the life of the Christian communion with the Triune God the Spirit glorifies the Lord Jesus Christ; the Spirit will take what is his and declare it to us (John 16:14-15):

— As Jesus reached out to all persons with his message of salvation and his caring love, so the Christian community is inclusive. No individual or group responding to Jesus' call to discipleship should be excluded from the community or, once inside, be made unimportant to its life and work. Still less should anyone be subjugated or dominated by those who are more powerful within the community.

— As Jesus related to an astonishing range of persons and refused to be bound by conventional standards of who is considered "acceptable", so the Christian community embraces and celebrates openness and diversity within its own life. Persons from all strands of life, those at the fringes and those at the centres of society, are accepted within the community of the body of Christ.

— As Jesus challenged all his followers to commit themselves to the kingdom and to bring their best gifts to its service, so the Christian community encourages the full participation of all its members and the development of the gifts of each. Men and women, old and young are given space to find their true identity as children of God.

— As Jesus called his followers to believe in the gospel, so the Christian community is one of growth in faith. But it understands that questioning, searching and doubt sometimes have their place within the process of growth.

— As Jesus called both men and women into his service, so the Christian community is one in which the gifts of both women and men are developed to the full, where members are not strangers to one another but brothers and sisters in the Lord. It is a community of love and friendship where human sexuality is neither ignored nor abused, but affirmed as God's gift in creation.

— As Jesus proclaimed that one receives life by losing it, so the Christian community is characterized by self-giving, mutual self-sacrifice, and love. It is a community of persons of equal worth, without superiors and inferiors, those dominating and those dominated. It seeks to order its life accordingly, to find structures of authority and community discipline which embody this vision of justice in community.

— As Jesus turned to the sick and broken-hearted and bound their wounds, so the Christian community is one of healing of spirit, mind and body; and thus it is called to be a healing community within, and for, the wider human family.

— As Jesus called his followers on a pilgrimage into the future, so the Christian community, always imperfect, is one of growth in the Spirit, a community of forgiveness and empowerment where all persons are accepted as they are and challenged to become fully what God wants them to be.

— As Jesus strengthened his followers by proclaiming God's word and instituting in their midst his meal of forgiveness, thanksgiving and communion, so the Christian community, in the power of the Holy Spirit, will be sustained and renewed by these means of God's grace. Here are its deepest well-springs for becoming a sign of justice and community for all humanity, until that perfect justice and communion will be celebrated in the Kingdom of God.

The marks of Christian community may vary... what is fundamental is a pattern of the community seeking the source and goal of its life in Christ, and of persistent caring, in the spirit of Christ, for others both in the community and in the world

---

Questions for Reflection and Discussion

1. What questions about language have arisen in your community or church? How are you dealing with them?

2. Do you experience the structures of authority in your church as empowering or not? What changes would you like to make?

3. Do you agree with this chapter's description of Christian community? Are there points which you would like to alter or to add?

CHAPTER VII

Unity and Renewal:
Eschatological Promise

Rejoice in your hope,
be patient in tribulation
be constant in prayer

Romans 12:12

1. Throughout this study the controlling motifs of *unity* and *renewal* in relation to the church and human community have been related to the promises of God as focussed in the kingdom. In this study document, the following affirmations have been made; rooted in Christian hope, they call for Christian action.

— The complete realization of the rule of God has still to come. God has the final word. The future belongs to God.

— The church as mystery came to birth that it might be the prophetic sign and effective instrument of the kingdom of God. The church is not the kingdom, but the promises of the kingdom are present in it.

— As mystery and prophetic sign the church must act on behalf of that justice which is a constitutive aspect of the reign of God. The specific contribution of Christians will be to apply the principles of the life and teaching of Jesus Christ, who as a just man hung and died on the cross (cf. Luke 23:47), to the concrete situations of injustice in today's world. And the church must express justice within its own life, so as to be a sign and promise of the eschatological kingdom of justice which is yet to be.

— The church must proclaim in word and in deed the fundamental equality of women and men, created in the image of God and now called to maturity in the image of Christ the first-born of all creation, the first-born of the dead who reconciles all in himself (cf.

Col. 1:15-20, 28). The church must be a community in which power is used to serve and not arbitrarily to exclude others, which fosters relationships of mutuality and communion, which promotes the full exercise of the charisms poured out upon the people of God, and which corrects the ways in which the use of language perpetuates prejudice and inequality.

— The vision of the coming kingdom of God judges individual Christians and congregations. We are called to repentance and offered the gift of grace that renews. This renewal is never for our sake alone. It is for the sake of the renewal of human community by making the church a more effective sign and instrument. In this renewal the church and the world stand alongside each other.

— The judgment that the vision of the kingdom of God delivers on the church reveals the truth concerning our disunity. The divisions within and between churches are demonic forces that diminish the church's effectiveness as sign and instrument.

— The gift of unity will surprise the church, for this unity will be manifested when, in faithfulness to the promises of God, the church serves the world in which it is set.

2. This dimension of Christian hope, rooted in the promises of God, is our source of joy even in tribulations and an encouragement to the life of prayer. The threefold pattern of hope, patience in tribulation, and prayer helps to focus our concluding doxological reflections.

1. Rejoice in your Hope

3. Christians proclaim in the second article of the Nicene Creed that "He will come again in glory." In proclaiming that Christ will come again we affirm our faith that history will not end in chaos, but in the one in whom it had its beginning, the one who is the Alpha and the Omega.

> To those who ask "What is coming to the world?" we answer "His kingdom is coming". To those who ask "What is in front of us?" we answer "It is He, the king, who confronts us". To those who ask "What may we look forward to?" we answer that we face not a trackless waste of unfilled time with an end that none can dare to predict; we face our living Lord, our Judge and Saviour, He who was dead and is alive for evermore, He who has come and is coming and will reign for ever and ever.
>
> *Christ — The Hope of the World*, p. 7

4. There is nevertheless a tension between the inauguration of the kingdom of Christ and its final fulfilment. The salvation worked in individual Chris-

tians is only part of the longed-for redemption of the whole creation. So Christians wait in eager hope for the final consummation of God's offer of new life, given to our world history in the resurrection of Christ, the crucified Lord.

5. This perspective of hope is expressed particularly strongly in the last book of the Bible, the book of Revelation. Its eschatological promise is related to every human person in his or her personal pain: "He will wipe away every tear from your eyes, and death shall be no more, neither shall there be mourning nor crying nor pain any more..." (Rev. 21:4). Yet not only individual persons but also human communities are seen in the light of hope. The vision of the "holy city", the "new Jerusalem", and, ultimately, of a "new heaven and a new earth" illuminates and instructs our responsibility and hope. This is no utopian vision. We are not the architects of the new Jerusalem; it is not a city made by human beings. It is the city of God. It is God's voice that utters the promise: "Behold, I make all things new" (Rev. 21:5). Once this promise sets us free we can begin our pilgrim way, setting out in the direction of the kingdom without utopian illusions, yet with joyful hope. God has the final word. The future belongs to God. The final judgment is God's.

6. The theme of judgment and repentance has been prominent in our understanding of the twin motifs of unity and of renewal in relation to the church. Christians proclaim at this point in the creed that Christ "will judge the living and the dead". All of us will have to appear before the judgment of Christ. This makes us humble. However the vision of the last judgment makes us also confident that the cause of justice, so often perverted in our sinful world, will be upheld and restored before God. Murderers will not ultimately triumph over their victims.

7. However much justice and love may be in tension in human life, the full witness of the Bible is that in God they cannot be separated. Human beings are not righteous, but our judge is the righteous one. Human beings cannot escape responsibility for sin, but they can face judgment trusting in God's merciful and forgiving love, that love revealed in Christ who himself has gone through suffering and vindication and pleads on our behalf as we stand before God.

8. The second article of the Nicene Creed finishes by proclaiming that Christ's "kingdom will have no end". The risen Christ is exalted to the right hand of God the Father, wielding the power of his kingdom. Although this will become apparent only at the time of his second coming, the church affirms it as a reality even now, hidden from our eyes, but effective nonetheless. This is our hope and joy.

2. Be Patient in Tribulation

9. Christians share with the rest of humanity the brokenness of this world with its consequent injustice, suffering and pain, but with the crucial difference that we have been incorporated into Christ by baptism and so share in

his sufferings and the subsequent glory. "The world" has oppressed and caused suffering to individual members of the church, congregations and whole Christian churches. Indeed, this is taking place at the present time in various parts of the world. Suffering is and remains one of the characteristic marks of the church of Jesus Christ, who himself suffered for our sake that we might share in the kingdom of God.

10. Through such suffering the church follows in the footsteps of the suffering servant. Such suffering should not be "spiritualised" (in the false sense of denying its concrete reality); nevertheless there is in it a hidden mystery, an eschatological reality. This is acknowledged in the statement that "the blood of the martyrs is the seed of the church". There is evidence even today that in many situations in which Christians are oppressed and experience suffering their faith and hope in the kingdom of God has not been extinguished but, on the contrary, has been strengthened and encouraged. At the Harlem Consultation the African American Churches witnessed to their experience of this truth:

> In a most important manner, mystery is expressed apocalyptically as a reversal of fortune in which "nobodies" in the estimation of society will become "somebodies" through God's action... In worship African-Americans experience how the "last can be first", how oppressed can be victorious, how broken bodies can be transformed into a victorious people... The African-American Church is a sign that the wider church often refuses to see; yet it points to the mystery of God, the power of God to transform and empower a people who have been despised and rejected... It is a sign to call the church to unity and to point out ways to human renewal... "The Lord will make a way somehow"...
>
> Harlem Consultation Report, pp. 3, 5, 6;
> *Mid-Stream*, XXVIII, 4, pp. 414, 416, 417

11. The very existence of the church in the midst of so much distress and trouble should be a sign to the world that it will never be left without God's sustaining power, and the church itself has been assured "that the powers of death shall not prevail against it" (Matt. 16:18).

12. As the Christian community gathers to worship God and to celebrate the eucharist, it experiences the reality of the kingdom of God, a reality which is effective though hidden. In and through the eucharist the Christian community becomes a communion, a fellowship of hope in which, by the power of the Holy Spirit, renewal is experienced as reconciliation, peace and justice, which are to be realised in the community and its witness to the world. Thus the church is a sign of God's future renewal of humanity. But at the same time the church looks forward to the consummation of the kingdom that is yet to come, for its own and the world's fulfilment. The church's hope is thus a hope for the whole world, and its trust is in God's redemptive promise of faithfulness to his entire creation.

3. Be Constant in Prayer

> Thy kingdom come.
> On bended knee the passing ages pray:
> and faithful souls have yearned to see on earth
> that kingdom's day.

From a hymn by F.L. Hosmer

13. Christians pray daily in the Lord's prayer, "Your kingdom come." While we live in a church and world in which there is disunity, the hope is expressed that the kingdom of God may grasp Christians and become a tangible reality. The fact that Christians repeat the Lord's prayer constantly shows that in their experience there is a dimension of waiting, active waiting upon God.

14. From praying, listening, and loving God emerges the determination to rid the world of injustice and brokenness. Contemplation and struggle, prayer and redeeming action are linked responses towards the unity of the church and the renewal of human community.

We need increasingly to realize that the separate histories of our Churches find their full meaning only if seen in the perspective of God's dealings with His *whole* people... A faith in the one Church of Christ which is not implemented by *acts* of obedience is dead... Should not our churches... act together in all matters except those in which deep differences of conviction compel them to act separately?

Third World Conference on Faith and Order, Lund, 1952

---

15. Through prayer Christians are empowered by God to overcome anxieties about the future and are set free to hope and to work for a more humane and just world.

16. From the activity of personal prayer and worship in the fellowship of the Christian community, Christians are filled with hope in the midst of a world that seems to deny the possibility of the kingdom of God. In spite of their weakness and fears they can live with confidence and trust in the promises of God.

17. *And so we pray*: Let thanks and praise be given to God the Father, in whose kingly rule we trust. In the promise of a new heaven and a new earth perfected according to your will, all the nations will come with their varied gifts and through your love the barriers and brokenness which separate and destroy peace will be overcome.

— That peace "in Christ" which passes all understanding will perfect relationships and bring harmony to your creation.

— May your power surprise and astonish us.

18. *And so we pray*: Let thanks and praise be given to God the Son, in whose resurrection and exaltation we share and glimpse the nature of the renewed humanity, a humanity which exceeds our imagination and expectations.

— May your faithfulness to the mission which God the Father gave you be our example and guide.

19. *And so we pray*: Let thanks and praise be given to God the Holy Spirit, in whose creative power we share. In your power to bring to perfection all that is, let us share. In your power to open eyes and ears, let us share. In your generous creativity, let us rejoice.

— Maranatha.

— Alleluia. Alleluia. Alleluia.

Texts and Materials Related to the Study Document

1. Consultation Reports and Papers, Related Materials

Chantilly, France Consultation (January, 1985): Report, "The Unity of the Church and the Renewal of Human Community: The Church as Mystery and Prophetic Sign", FO/85:4, Latest Revision: October 1988. (First draft, Chantilly, January 1985; second draft, Stavanger, August 1985; further revisions March 1986, July 1987). (Latest German text: "Die Kirche als Mysterium und Prophetisches Zeichen", Rev. Fassung März 1986/July 1987 [Revision of July, 1987]). The consultation papers and first version of the report are published in Gennadios Limouris, ed., *Church, Kingdom, World*, Faith and Order Paper No. 130, Geneva, WCC, 1986, Report: pp. 163-175.

Prague, Czechoslovakia Consultation (September-October, 1985): Papers and the Report published in Thomas F. Best, ed., *Beyond Unity-in-Tension: Unity, Renewal and the Community of Women and Men*, Faith and Order Paper No. 138, Geneva, WCC, 1988, Report: pp. 159-163. See also: Martin Cressey, "A Personal Theological/Ecclesiological Reflection on the Prague Consultation", pp. 147-158, and Thomas F. Best: "Beyond Unity-In-Tension — Prague: The Issues and the Experience in Ecumenical Perspective", pp. 1-33.

Singapore Consultation (November, 1986): Report, "Unity and Renewal: The Ecclesiological Significance of the churches' Involvement in Issues of Justice", FO/87:13. The Report and most papers are published in Paul A. Crow, Jr. and Thomas F. Best, eds., "Justice, Unity and Renewal: The Search for Visible Unity and the churches' Involvement in Issues of Justice", a thematic issue of *Mid-stream*, Vol. XXVIII, No. 1, January, 1989, Report: pp. 85-102. Two of the papers are published in Thomas F. Best, ed., "Unity and Mission: An Ecumenical Challenge", a special issue of *The Ecumenical Review*, Vol. 39, No. 3, July, 1987. The quotation in Chapter IV, para. 21 on page 45 of this Study Document is from Felix Wilfred, "Action Groups and the Struggle for Justice in India: Ecclesiological Implications" [paper presented to the Singapore consultation], in *The Ecumenical Review*, Vol. 39, No. 3, July, 1987, pp. 291-309. The paper referred to in Chapter IV, para. 28 on page 47 of this

Study Document is from Padmasani Gallup, "Casteism in the church — A Case Study" [paper presented to the Singapore consultation], in *Mid-Stream*, XXVIII, No. 1, January, 1989, pp. 1-11.

Porto Alegre, Brazil Consultation (November, 1987): Report, "Unity of the church and Renewal of Human Community: The Ecclesiological Significance of the churches' Involvement in Issues of Justice", FO/87:37 Rev., February 1988. Published with the consultation papers in Paul A. Crow, Jr. and Thomas F. Best, eds., "Justice, Unity and Renewal: The Search for Visible Unity and the churches' Involvement in Issues of Justice", a thematic issue of *Mid-stream*, Vol. XXVIII, No. 1, January, 1989, Report: pp. 103-114. (Spanish: "Unidad y Renovación: Informes de las Consultas de Porto Alegre, Brasil", Edición en Español para America Latina, Centro de Estudios Cristianos, Buenos Aires, 1988; also published as "El Significado Eclesiológico del Compromiso de las Iglesias en el Tema de la Justicia", *Cuadernos de Teologia*, IX, No. 2, 1988, pp. 218-228. Portugese: "A Unidade de Igreja e a Renovação da Comunidade Humana: O Significado Eclesiologico do Envolvimento das Igrejas em Questões de Justiça", 1988.)

Harlem, USA Consultation (August, 1988): Report, "Unity and Renewal/Black Churches in the United States of America Consultation", FO/88:42. Published with the consultation papers in Paul A. Crow, Jr., ed., *Mid-Stream*, Vol. XXVIII, No. 4, October, 1989; editorial introduction by Thomas F. Best, pp. 333-335; papers, pp. 336-368; Report, pp. 412-420. The quotation in Chapter IV, para. 29 on page 47 of this Study Document is from Preston Williams, *et al.*, "An African-American Perspective on the Unity of the Church and the Renewal of Human Community" [paper presented to the Harlem Consultation], p. 8; see *Mid-Stream*, Vol. XXVIII, No. 4, October, 1989, p. 342.

Porto Novo, Benin Consultation (September, 1988): Report, "The Ecclesiological Significance of the Community of Women and Men", FO/88:44, Report and papers to be published. The quotation in Chapter VI, para. 10 on pages 66-67 of this Study Document is from Arnold Temple, "The Ecclesiological Significance of the Community of Women and Men: An African Perspective" [paper presented to the Benin Consultation], p. 3.

Unity and Renewal: A Study Guide for Local Groups. Faith and Order Paper No. 136, Geneva, WCC, 1987 (Spanish: *Unidad y Renovación*, Edicion en Español para America Latina, Centro de Estudios Cristianos, Buenos Aires, 1987).

Thomas F. Best, compiler, "Unity and Renewal — A Working Bibliography", 26 July 1990.

2. Faith and Order Commission and Unity and Renewal Steering Group Meetings

Montreal (1963): "Scripture, Tradition and traditions" in P. C. Rodger and L. Vischer, eds., *The Fourth World Conference on Faith and Order: Montreal, 1963*, Faith and Order Paper No. 42, London, SCM Press Ltd, 1964, pp. 50-61.

Lima (1982): Related papers and group reports in Michael Kinnamon, ed., *Towards Visible Unity*, Vols. I and II, Faith and Order Paper Nos. 112 and 113, Geneva, WCC, 1982, Vol. I, pp. 111-124; Vol. II, pp. 123-130.

Crete (1984): "The Unity of the Church and the Renewal of Human Community: Programme Outline", in *Commission on Faith and Order: Minutes of the Meeting of the Standing Commission, 1984, Crete*, Faith and Order Paper No. 121, Geneva, WCC, 1984, pp. 33-52.

Stavanger (1985): Related papers and group reports in Thomas F. Best, ed., *Faith and Renewal: Commission on Faith and Order, Stavanger 1985*, Faith and Order Paper No. 131, Geneva, WCC, 1986, pp. 107-114, 166-221.

Potsdam (1986): "Unity and Renewal", in *Minutes of the Meeting of the Standing Commission, 1986, Potsdam, GDR*, Faith and Order Paper No. 134, Geneva, WCC, 1986, pp. 42-45.

Madrid (1987): "The Unity of the Church and the Renewal of Human Community", in *Minutes of the Meeting of the Standing Commission, 1987, Madrid, Spain*, Faith and Order Paper No. 141, Geneva, WCC, 1987, pp. 14-15, 83-89.

Boston (1988): "The Unity of the Church and the Renewal of Human Community: Report", in *Minutes of the Meeting of the Standing Commission, 1988, Boston, USA*, Faith and Order Paper No. 145, Geneva, Faith and Order Commission, WCC, 1988, pp. 10-14, 97-99.

Budapest (1989): Related papers and group reports in Thomas F. Best, ed., *Faith and Order 1985-1989: The Commission Meeting at Budapest 1989*, Faith and Order Paper No. 148, Geneva, WCC, 1990, pp. 134-162.

Leuenberg, Switzerland (1989): "The Unity of the Church and the Renewal of Human Community: A Study Document for the churches" (FO/89:6).

Mandeville, Jamaica (1990): "Church and World: The Unity of the Church and the Renewal of Human Community" (FO/89:6 rev.).

Dunblane, Scotland (1990): "Report from the Unity and Renewal Steering Group: Revisions of the Study Document", in *Minutes of the Meeting of the Standing Commission, 1990, Dunblane, Scotland*, Faith and Order Paper No. 152, Geneva, Faith and Order Commission, WCC, 1988, see pp. 54-58.

3. Additional Sources

Baptism, Eucharist and Ministry, Faith and Order Paper No. 111, Geneva, WCC, 1982.

Thomas F. Best, ed., *Living Today Towards Visible Unity: The Fifth International Consultation of United and Uniting Churches* [Potsdam, 1987], Faith and Order Paper No. 142, Geneva, WCC, 1988, Report, pp. 3-20. German text: Thomas F. Best, hrsg., *Gemeinsam auf dem Weg zur sichtbaren Einheit*, Berlin (West), Kirchenkanzlei der Evangelischen Kirche der Union, 1988.

Christ — The Hope of the World [Documents on the Main Theme of the Second WCC Assembly, Evanston, 1954], Geneva, World Council of Churches, 1954.

"Constitution and Rules of the WCC", in *Gathered for Life*, pp. 324-347.

David Gill, ed., *Gathered for Life* [WCC Sixth Assembly, Vancouver, 1983], Geneva and Grand Rapids, WCC and Wm. B. Eerdmans, 1983.

F. L. Hosmer, "Thy Kingdom Come", in *Hymns Ancient and Modern*, New Standard Edition, Hymns Ancient and Modern, Ltd., Norwich, 1983, No. 178.

Inter Insigniores: Declaration on the Question of the Admission of Women to the Ministerial Priesthood, Rome, Sacred Congregation for the Doctrine of the Faith, 27 January, 1977.

Nairobi to Vancouver: 1975-1983, Report of the Central Committee to the Sixth Assembly of the World Council of Churches, Geneva, WCC, 1983.

"The Place of the Woman in the Orthodox Church and the Question of the Ordination of Women" [Report of the Ecumenical Patriarchate Inter-Orthodox Theological Consultation, Rhodes, Greece, 30 October - 7 November 1988], Istanbul, Ecumenical Patriarchate, 1988.

"Report of the Core Group on Unit I", WCC Core Group Meeting, Montreux, Switzerland, January, 1984. [See also: "Working Paper to the Core Group of the Programme Unit on Faith and Witness".]

Your Kingdom Come: Mission Perspectives. Report on the World Conference on Mission and Evangelism, 1980, Geneva, WCC/CWME, 1980.

For The Community of Women and Men in the Church study programme (1977-1981) see the following:

"The Authority of Scripture" [Report of a Consultation on "The Authority of Scripture in Light of the New Experiences of Women" (Amsterdam, 1980)], in Janet Crawford and Michael Kinnamon, *In God's Image: Reflections on Identity, Human Wholeness and the Authority of Scripture*, Geneva, WCC, 1983, pp. 79-108.

Janet Crawford, "Identity", in Janet Crawford and Michael Kinnamon, *In God's Image: Reflections on Identity, Human Wholeness and the Authority of Scripture*, Geneva, WCC, 1983, pp. 1-46.

Constance F. Parvey, ed., *The Community of Women and Men in the Church: The Sheffield Report*, Geneva, WCC, 1981.

- German: Constance F. Parvey, hrsg., *Die Gemeinschaft von Frauen und Männern in der Kirche*, transl. by Elisabeth Raiser and Verena Coenen, Neukirchener-Vluyn, Neukirchener Verlag, 1985.

- Italian: Constance F. Parvey, ed., *La Comunita delle Donne e degli Uomini nella Chiesa*, transl. by Mirella Corsani, Torino, Editrice Elle di Ci, Editrice Claudiana, 1984.

Constance F. Parvey, ed., *Ordination of Women in Ecumenical Perspective: Workbook for the Church's Future* [based on a consultation at Klingenthal, 1979] Faith and Order Paper No. 105, Geneva, WCC, 1980.

Study on the Community of Women and Men in the church: A Study Guide, Geneva, WCC, Faith and Order/Sub-Unit on Women, 1978 [published in various countries in other languages; reports from several regional consultations using the Study Guide were also received].

Betty Thompson, *A Chance to Change: Women and Men in the Church*, Risk Books, Geneva, WCC, 1982.

"Wholeness" [Report of a Consultation on "Towards a Theology of Human Wholeness" (Niederaltaich, 1980)], in Janet Crawford and Michael Kinnamon, *In God's Image: Reflections on Identity, Human Wholeness and the Authority of Scripture*, Geneva, WCC, 1983, pp. 47-78.

For the Ecumenical Decade of the Churches in Solidarity with Women (1988—1998) see the following:

Decade Link, Sub-unit on Women in Church and Society, Geneva, WCC, published occasionally.

"Ecumenical Decade: The Churches in Solidarity with Women, 1988-1998", Sub-unit on Women in Church and Society, Geneva, WCC, 1988.

Anna Karin Hammar and Anne-Marie Käppeli, eds., "Prayers & Poems, Songs & Stories", special issue of *Women in a Changing World*, 25, January, 1988.

4. References for the "Illustrative" Material

Page 3: "Final Document of the European Ecumenical Assembly 'Peace with Justice/Peace with Justice for the Whole Creation'" (Basel, 1989) , para. 45, in *Peace with Justice*, Geneva, Conference of European Churches, 1989, pp. 47-48.

Page 11: (Anglican) Bishop T. S. A. Annobil of Ghana, speaking of experiences related to the Faith and Order text *Baptism, Eucharist and Ministry*.

Page 18: "Final Document: 'Entering into Covenant Solidarity for Justice, Peace and the Integrity of Creation'", World Convocation (Seoul, March 1990), Affirmation I.

Page 23: *Confessing The One Faith* [Text from Apostolic Faith study programme], to be published in 1991, para. 237.

Page 24: Cardinal Roger Etchegaray, "Peace with Justice for the Whole Creation: Christian Responsibility in a Time of Crisis", in *Peace with Justice*, Geneva, Conference of European Churches, 1989, p. 208.

Page 32: John Zizioulas, "The local church in a eucharistic perspective - an Orthodox contribution", in *In Each Place: Towards a Fellowship of Local Churches Truly United*, Geneva, WCC, 1977, p. 56.

Page 42: John Chrysostom on Matthew: Homily 50.4, translation based on LF 15.684-685, quoted from W. J. Burghardt, "The Body of Christ: Patristic Insights", in R. S. Pelton, ed., *The Church as the Body of Christ*, South Bend, 1963.

Page 43: St. Augustine, "Sermon on the Christian Life".

Page 59: Flora Winfield describing the Oxford Women's Liturgy Group.

Page 61: *Baptism, Eucharist and Ministry*, Faith and Order Paper No. 111, Geneva, WCC, 1982, "Ministry", para. 54

Page 65: Statement by an El Salvadoran woman on Mother's Day, 1983, in Hans-Georg Link, ed., *Confessing Our Faith Around the World, III: The Caribbean and Central America*, Faith and Order Paper No. 123, Geneva, WCC, 1984, p. 21. Text from "Latinamerica Press", 14 July 1983.

Page 67: Julian of Norwich, *Revelations of Divine Love*, Chapter 60.

Page 70: *Epistle to Diognetus*, 10.2, ECS 181.

Page 78: *Faith and Order: The Report of the Third World Conference at Lund, Sweden: August 15-28, 1952*, Faith and Order Paper No. 15, London, SCM Press, 1952, pp. 5-6 [Chapter I, "A Word to the Churches", paras. 2 - 3].

5. Photo Identifications and Credits

Page 8: Taizé, Easter 1972.

Page 9: Berlin — Ostbahnhof. Photo Heinz Wenzel, Berlin.

Page 10: Eucharist at Lutheran World Federation VIIth Assembly, Budapest 1984. LWF photo by Tibor Moldovanyi.

Page 15: Methodist worship near Gweru, Zimbabwe. WCC photo: Peter Williams.

Page 20: The Last Supper (1982), print by Sadao Watanabe. Used with permission.

Page 28: WCC photo: Peter Williams.

Page 29: "Christians for Peace": offering public Christian witness in Madrid. WCC photo: Peter Williams.

Page 41: Resident of Mississippi, U.S.A., voting in 1967. Delta Ministry photo by Nash Basom.

Page 46: Roman Catholic Archbishop Helder Pessoa Camara, Diocese of Olinda and Recife, Brazil. Photo: United Methodist Board of Global Ministries. Used with permission.

Page 52: Worship in St Barabas Cathedral (Church of Melanesia [Anglican]), Solomon Islands, 1986. WCC photo: Peter Williams.

Page 57: Confirmation by Pastor Una Jarn in Kildevaeld Church, Copenhagen, Denmark, 1985. The painting behind the altar depicts Jesus' encounter with the Samaritan woman at the well (John 4:7-26). WCC photo: Peter Williams.

Page 68: Worship in a Presbyterian chapel in Chimaltenanco, Guatemala, 1986. WCC photo: Peter Williams.

Page 71: "Moleben" (thanksgiving service) at Zagorsk (Russian Orthodox monastic centre), 18 July 1989. WCC photo: Peter Williams.

Page 79: Photo by John P. Taylor, Oikumene.

6. Note on Biblical Translation

The translation of Revelation 5:6-10 used on p. 14 of this Study Document is that of G. B. Caird, *The Revelation of St John the Divine*, Black's New Testament Commentaries, Adam & Charles Black, London, 1966, see pp. 69-77.

The Unity and Renewal Consultations/Steering Group Meetings

1. "The Church as Mystery and Prophetic Sign". Chantilly, France. January 1985.

2. "Unity and Renewal and the Community of Women and Men". Prague, Czechoslovakia. September 1985.

3. "The Ecclesiological Significance of the churches' Involvement in Issues of Justice". Singapore. November 1986.

4. "The Ecclesiological Significance of the churches' Involvement in Issues of Justice". Porto Alegre, Brazil. November 1987.

5. "Unity and Renewal/Black Churches in the United States of America Consultation". Harlem, USA. August 1988.

6. "Unity and Renewal and Issues of Justice: Insights and Reflections". Boston, USA. September 1988. (Drafting meeting of the Steering Group).

7. "The Ecclesiological Significance of the Community of Women and Men". Porto Novo, Benin. September 1988.

8. "Unity and Renewal and Issues of the Community of Women and Men: Insights and Reflections". Cambridge, U.K. January 1989. (Drafting meeting, and review of initial local group results, with members of the Steering Group and others).

9. "Unity and Renewal: Towards a Draft Report". Leuenberg, Switzerland. March 1989. (Drafting meeting of the Steering Group and advisors).

10. "Unity and Renewal: Towards a Final Text". Mandeville, Jamaica. January 1990. (Drafting meeting of the Steering Group and advisors).

11. In addition, important work was done at gatherings of the Unity and Renewal Steering Group in connection with meetings of the Faith and Order Standing Commission (Crete, March 1984; Potsdam, GDR, July 1986; Madrid, Spain, August 1987; Boston, USA, September 1988) and Plenary Commission (Stavanger, Norway, August 1985; Budapest, August 1989).

12. Final revision by the Steering Group, and approval of the text *Church and World: The Unity of the Church and the Renewal of Human Community* for publication, distribution and study by the churches, took place at the Faith and Order Standing Commission meeting in Dunblane, Scotland, August 1990.

The Unity and Renewal Steering Group and Staff

1. The Unity and Renewal Steering Group

Rev. Dr. Paul A. Crow, Jr., Moderator (Christian Church - Disciples of Christ, USA)

Rt. Rev. John Austin Baker (Church of England, England) (Steering Group member through 1986)

Protopresbyter Vitaly Borovoy (Russian Orthodox, USSR)

Rt. Rev. Manas Buthelezi (Lutheran, South Africa)

Rev. Janet Crawford (Anglican, Aotearoa/New Zealand)

Rev. Martin H. Cressey (United Reformed Church in the United Kingdom, England)

Archbishop Aram Keshishian (Armenian Apostolic Church, Lebanon)

Prof. Jan M. Lochman (Swiss Protestant Church Federation, Switzerland)

Rev. Augustina Lumentut (Christian Church in Central Sulawesi, Indonesia)

Dr. Mercy Amba Oduyoye (Methodist, Ghana) (Steering Group member through 1988)

Rev. Aracely E. de Rochietti (Methodist Church, Uruguay)

Rt. Rev. Barry Rogerson (Church of England, England)

Rt. Rev. Paul-Werner Scheele (Roman Catholic, Germany)

Prof. Gayraud Wilmore (Presbyterian Church (U.S.A.), USA)

2. The Following Were Also Involved in the Final Drafting Process

A. At Leuenberg

Rev. Dr. S.T. Ola Akande (Baptist, Nigeria)

Very Rev. Prof. Emmanuel Clapsis (Greek Orthodox Archidiocese of North and South America/Ecumenical Patriarchate, USA)

Rev. Dr. Ioan Dura (Romanian Orthodox, Belgium)

Rev. Beverly Gaventa (Disciples of Christ, USA)

Rev. William Henn, OFM Cap (Roman Catholic, Italy)

Dr. Thomas Hoyt (Christian Methodist Episcopal, USA)

Father Hervé Legrand, O.P. (Roman Catholic, France)

B. AT MANDEVILLE

Very Rev. Prof. Emmanuel Clapsis (Greek Orthodox Archidiocese of North
  and South America/Ecumenical Patriarchate, USA)
Rev. William Henn, OFM Cap (Roman Catholic, Italy)
Rev. Dr. Horace O. Russell (Jamaica Baptist Union, Jamaica)

C. AT DUNBLANE

Rev. Dr. Lothar Coenen (Evangelical Church in Germany: United, Germany)

3. Faith and Order Staff Involved in the Unity and Renewal Study

Rev. Dr. Thomas F. Best (Christian Church - Disciples of Christ, USA) —
  executive staff responsible for the Unity and Renewal study
Mrs. Eileen Chapman (Uniting Church in Australia, Australia) — Adminis-
  trative Assistant for the Unity and Renewal study
Rev. Dr. Günther Gassmann (Evangelical Church in Germany: Lutheran,
  Germany) — Director, Faith and Order
Rev. Dr. Irmgard Kindt-Siegwalt (Evangelical Church in Germany: Luth-
  eran, Germany) — Benin and Cambridge consultations
V. Rev. Prof. Dr Gennadios Limouris (Ecumenical Patriarchate, Greece) —
  Chantilly and Prague consultations

Overview of the Study Process

THE UNITY OF THE CHURCH
AND THE RENEWAL OF HUMAN COMMUNITY

The Study Process

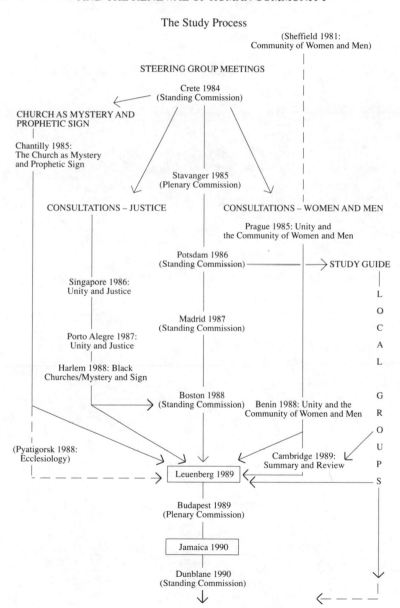

(Sheffield 1981:
Community of Women and Men)

STEERING GROUP MEETINGS

Crete 1984
(Standing Commission)

CHURCH AS MYSTERY AND
PROPHETIC SIGN

Chantilly 1985:
The Church as Mystery
and Prophetic Sign

Stavanger 1985
(Plenary Commission)

CONSULTATIONS – JUSTICE

CONSULTATIONS – WOMEN AND MEN

Prague 1985: Unity and
the Community of Women and Men

Potsdam 1986
(Standing Commission) ————————→ STUDY GUIDE

Singapore 1986:
Unity and Justice

L

O

Madrid 1987
(Standing Commission)

C

Porto Alegre 1987:
Unity and Justice

A

L

Harlem 1988: Black
Churches/Mystery and Sign

Boston 1988
(Standing Commission)

G

Benin 1988: Unity and the
Community of Women and Men

R

O

(Pyatigorsk 1988:
Ecclesiology)

Cambridge 1989:
Summary and Review

U

Leuenberg 1989

P

S

Budapest 1989
(Plenary Commission)

Jamaica 1990

Dunblane 1990
(Standing Commission)